KID KITCHEN

Fun & Easy Recipes

You Can Make All by Yourself!

(or With Just a Little Help)

KID KITCHEN

HEATHER STALLER

Author of *Little Helpers Toddler Cookbook*
and Founder of Happy Kids Kitchen

PAGE STREET
PUBLISHING CO.

PAGE STREET
PUBLISHING CO.

First published in 2023 by
Page Street Publishing Co.
27 Congress Street, Suite 1511
Salem, MA 01970
www.pagestreetpublishing.com

Distributed by Macmillan, sales in Canada by The Canadian Manda Group.

27 26 25 24 23   1 2 3 4 5

ISBN-13: 978-1-64567-720-8
ISBN-10: 1-64567-720-6

Library of Congress Control Number: 2022945189

Cover and book design by Rosie Stewart for Page Street Publishing Co.
Photography by Michelle Boule, additional photo and design elements from
Shutterstock

Printed and bound in the United States of America

Page Street Publishing protects our planet by donating to nonprofits like
The Trustees, which focuses on local land conservation.

DEDICATION

To Jack, Henry and all the other young chefs
out there (like you!), making the world
a more delicious place.

CONTENTS

INTRODUCTION

Hey, friend. Welcome! We're about to have some serious fun cooking snacks and meals that will have you feeling like a rock star.

Cooking is the adventure of a lifetime. I started cooking at your age, just like you! I still remember getting my first cookbook. Like the one you're holding, it was full of bright, colorful photos, and I was so excited to make MY OWN meals and desserts.

One day, I had a friend over, and we picked out the teriyaki chicken to make ourselves for dinner. We read the recipe, measured, mixed the sweet sauce and placed the chicken on the stove to cook. What seemed like a few minutes later, I could smell that something wasn't quite right. We lifted the lid, and under the puff of smoke was a thick, BLACK layer of sludge covering the bottom of the pan. It was so burnt! We managed to salvage the top of the chicken, and it actually didn't taste that bad.

Even though I was disappointed in myself for not paying closer attention to the pan and heat level of the stove, the excitement to keep trying new recipes and get better at cooking burned even brighter. I spent the next 20+ years watching every Food Network show on TV, reading every food magazine on the shelves and eventually, finding such a passion for the art of cooking that I enrolled in culinary school.

Here's the thing about cooking: There's always more to learn and new ways to flex your creative muscles! There may be ups and downs, but the rewards of feeling proud of what you created, sharing delicious food with friends and family and improving your skills will keep you going.

I'm here to help you learn how to cook and make awesome food at the same time. So, let's start the adventure!

Heather ☺

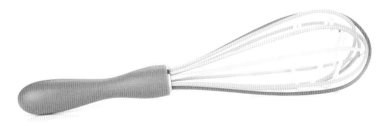

WHY COOKING IS ❀ AWESOME ❀

Make it YOUR WAY

No one knows your taste buds better than you! Once you master basic cooking skills, you can make adjustments and additions to recipes to make them exactly what you want to eat.

Sharing Is Caring

Nothing makes the people in your life happier than when you cook for them. You'll feel like a star when friends and family compliment and enjoy the food you've made.

Body Love

I know when you're a kid you don't think about what your body will feel like years down the road, but when you cook at home from scratch, you are much more likely to live a healthy life full of nourishing foods. Cooking is an important way to take care of your body!

Never Go Hungry

When you learn to cook for yourself, you'll be able to make a snack or meal with whatever ingredients are around.

☀ HOW TO USE THIS BOOK ☀

When choosing a recipe, think about how much time you have and how much effort you want to put into cooking at that moment. Are you looking for a fun, quick, after-school snack, or do you have a whole afternoon to cook up a delish family dinner?

Each recipe will say what level it is, so check that area when you are deciding what recipe you want to make. When you first start cooking from this book, try out a few Level 1 recipes so you get some practice before moving on and conquering the other levels.

Level 1: Easy-Peasy

» Only a few ingredients
» Simple steps and perfect for when you're short on time
» No (or very little) knives or heat

Level 2: Totally Doable

» More time and some knife skills needed
» May need an adult for help with the stove or oven

Level 3: Challenge Accepted!

» More time involved but totally worth it
» Use those knife skills!
» Grown-up supervision needed for the stove or oven

If you're wondering about ingredient substitutes for allergies or dietary needs, be sure to check out the Allergy Friendly Index on page 160. When possible, I'll list a way to adjust the recipe to fit your needs.

A NOTE TO GROWN-UP HELPERS

First, congratulations! I applaud you for embracing the child in your life's curiosity about cooking. As a mom to nine- and seven-year-old boys, I know firsthand that having kids in the kitchen can be stressful, nerve-wracking and/or messy (tips on that below!). However, the benefits far outweigh any initial drawbacks. While cooking, kids are practicing reading and math skills and seeing science play out in real-life situations. Cooking develops grit, creativity, problem-solving abilities and confidence. The pride on a child's face when they are sharing a self-made meal or treat with friends and family is priceless.

As a "grown-up helper," it's hard to know when to step in and help or step back and let the child figure it out. The kitchen has its dangers, and of course we never want our kids to get hurt. However, with time and practice, we can learn to trust our kids more and more as their own competency and confidence grow. You, too, are a rock star for encouraging and supporting this new generation of cooks and lifelong learners.

Ways to Prevent or Reduce THE MESS

» **Make a Kitchen Contract.** Take some time to sit down and talk about or write down the rules of your kitchen, including a cleanup checklist. Make the plan as specific as you can with clear expectations you can refer to as your child is learning the skill of cleaning up.

» **Teach "Clean as You Go."** It's much easier to wash a few dishes as you use them than it is facing a mountain of dishes after cooking. Discuss and demonstrate what that looks like.

» **Make it FUN.** Cleaning up is a drag, so encourage your child to put on their favorite music or set a timer to see how fast they can clean up.

Top Five Tips for Kitchen Safety

1. Squeaky Clean! Always wash your hands with warm water and soap before cooking. Wash your hands directly after touching any meat or chicken and cracking eggs to prevent illness.

2. Laser Focus! Don't try to multitask, because that's when accidents or mistakes happen. Always look down at your hands while using a knife or other tool.

3. Hot! Always use oven mitts to touch pans that have been on the stove or in the oven. You never know when a handle or other spot might be hot. Make sure your oven mitts are dry and don't have any holes.

4. High Five! Keep those fingers tucked under and out of the way. Even if you are using a child-safe knife or wearing a safety glove, it's always important to practice the proper form for when you do move on to a regular knife.

5. It's Always Okay to Ask for Help! You need practice in order for cooking skills—like chopping an apple or taking a pan out of the oven—to get easier. However, if something feels really tricky, it's better to ask for help than get hurt.

Top Tips to Be a Great Chef

1. Taste, Taste, Taste! You can't serve food to anyone without making sure it tastes good first. (When it's safe and not too hot, of course.)

2. Season! When something tastes bland, it usually needs a little more salt. Also, a little squeeze of lemon juice is always a good idea to brighten up the flavor of any dish.

3. You Can Always Add but You Can't Take Away. Sprinkle in a little seasoning at a time (or anything else) because you can always add more if you need to, but you can't take out an ingredient when you use too much of it.

4. Measurements Matter . . . Most of the Time. Especially when baking, you need to use the correct ingredients and amounts to get the best result. However, when you're not baking, or once you've mastered a recipe as written, don't be afraid to put your own spin on something.

5. The Best Kitchen Tool? Your Hands! Don't be afraid to mix, knead and prep food with your hands when it's safe and appropriate.

6. Use All Your Senses! Listen to how a hot pan sounds when you add a vegetable to it. Smell everything and pay close attention to how ingredients change and transform throughout the cooking process.

❧ CHEF'S TOOLBOX ❧

Measuring Cups and Spoons

Liquid Measuring Cup

Whisk

Chef Knife

Serrated Knife

Paring Knife

Knife Set

Rubber Spatula

Box Grater

Glass/Plastic Mixing Bowls

Small Prep Bowls

Microplane® Zester

Tongs

Wooden Spoon

Citrus Squeezer

Rolling Pin

Peeler

Pastry Brush

Garlic Press

Electric Hand Mixer

Pizza Wheel

Instant-Read Thermometer

Food Processor

Kitchen Scissors

Sauté Pan/Skillet

Blender

Sheet Pan/Baking Sheet

ESSENTIAL SKILLS TO COOK LIKE A ROCK-STAR CHEF

Knife skills

Choose the right knife for you. When you're new to using a knife, it's best to start practicing with a child-safe knife. Usually made from nylon or plastic, they are widely available online and are great for cutting many foods without the risk of cutting hands.

Once you're ready, move on to practicing with a paring knife or small chef's knife, depending on what you need to cut. Always pay close attention to your hands when using a knife, and tuck those fingers under and away!

Additionally, many recipes in this book call for using clean kitchen scissors, pizza wheels or graters to chop or cut foods. Use these tools with the same caution you would a knife.

Slice

Large Dice/ chop

Small Dice/ chop

Mince

Thin strips (Julienne)

Measuring Ingredients for Accuracy

Especially when baking, it's important to measure all of the ingredients accurately in order for the recipe you're making to come out right and taste great.

Measuring Cups

Full and flat! That's how the measuring cup should look when you measure dry ingredients such as flour, sugar and cocoa powder. You don't want the cup overflowing, and you don't want some of the cup empty.

Measuring Spoons

Scoop up the ingredient with the teaspoon (or measurement needed), and then use a very straight finger to level off the top. Make sure you don't dip into the spoon or you'll remove some of the ingredient and have too little.

The Best Way to Measure Flour

Use a spoon to fill the measuring cup so it's almost overflowing, and then scrape off the top with the back of a butter knife. This is called "leveling off" the top. Scooping the flour directly with the measuring cup can sometimes pack the flour into the cup and lead to extra flour being added to the recipe you're making. So, for the best results, use this "scoop and level" method!

Liquids

For water, milk or other liquid ingredients, it's best to use a liquid measuring cup. Crouch down and look at the measurements on the side of the cup at eye level to accurately measure the amount of liquid.

Seasoning Food Like a Pro

Learning the proper way to season food is an essential cooking skill because without seasoning, the food you cook won't taste good!

Chef's Sprinkle

When adding salt to a recipe, like when you are sprinkling salt over veggies on a baking sheet or to food in a pan, you take a big pinch of kosher salt with your fingers, raise the pinch high above the food and sprinkle it, moving your hand all around. Doing this ensures the salt is evenly distributed. Remember, especially when seasoning with salt, you can always add more after tasting, but it's very hard to fix a recipe that's too salty.

Zesting Citrus Fruit

The zest is the outside part of citrus fruit such as lemons, limes and oranges, and it has a lot of flavor. However, the pith, which is the white part right underneath the colorful zest, is bitter, and we don't want to eat that part. The best tool for removing the zest from fruit is called a Microplane® zester or grater. Carefully rub the zester over the citrus fruit so that the little "teeth" remove the zest. Keep moving around the fruit so that you don't grate the white pith under the skin. You can also use the smallest holes on a box grater if you don't have a special Microplane® zester.

Juicing Citrus Fruit

To get the most juice out of your citrus, first roll the fruit on the counter, pushing down on it to release the juices inside. After rolling, cut the fruit in half widthwise, and then use a juicing tool to squeeze the juice into a bowl. If you don't have a juicing tool, use your hands to juice the fruit into a bowl, and use a spoon to remove any seeds that might have fallen in.

Defrosting

In recipes where you need to use food that is frozen, such as vegetables, fruit or proteins, you can defrost it in a few different ways. For foods like fruits or vegetables, you can leave them out on the counter until they are soft and no longer frozen. In some cases, you can speed up the process by heating them in the microwave. (Try using a low power, such as 30 or 50 percent, so they defrost more evenly than regular high power.)

The safest way to defrost proteins such as meat or seafood while preventing foodborne illness is to place them on a plate in the refrigerator for a day until they are completely defrosted.

Master of the skillet

Whether it's a burger, pancake or grilled cheese, when you are flipping food from one side to the other, it's best to always turn the food away from you to prevent anything hot from splattering on you. You want to place the spatula all the way under the food, and then use your wrist to flip it up and towards the back of the pan. This skill takes practice!

Baking skills

Softening Butter

Many baking recipes call for softened butter, which means it is no longer cold or firm. If you plan ahead, you can leave a stick of butter out on the counter for 30 minutes to 1 hour, and it should be soft. To speed up the process, cut the butter into small pieces and leave it out on the counter. Butter is the right softness when you can press your finger into it and it leaves a soft imprint. If your finger can squish all the way through the butter super easily, it may be a little too soft (likely because your kitchen is very warm); try putting the butter back in the fridge for 5 minutes. Unless the recipe calls for melted butter, you do not want to soften butter in the microwave. Note: Some recipes in cookbooks call for butter at "room temperature"; this is the same as softened butter.

Baking Time

All ovens bake a little differently, so always set a timer for 5 minutes less than the baking time in the instructions. Look for the visual cues described in the recipe, such as the edges being golden brown, and then test for doneness (described below). If your food needs a little more time, set the timer for 5 minutes, or less, and check it again. Try to avoid opening the oven door more times than necessary. Each time you do, heat escapes, which can bring down the temperature of the oven and take the food longer to finish baking.

Testing Doneness

To tell when cake, muffins or any kind of baked good is cooked through, insert a toothpick or tip of a butter knife into the center. If it comes out clean, with no wet batter sticking to the toothpick or knife (a few moist crumbs are okay), the baked good is finished.

CULINARY DICTIONARY

Bake: To cook in an oven using dry heat, usually used when referring to cooking sweet foods like cookies and cakes.

Roast: Roasting is the same as baking. It simply means to cook in an oven using dry heat. However, we usually use the term "roast" when cooking savory foods like vegetables or meat.

Sauté: To cook in a pan using a little bit of fat (oil or butter) at medium to high heat.

stir-fry: Similar to sautéing, but with higher heat and continuous motion used to cook the food quickly.

Sear: To use high heat for a short period of time to "brown" meat, which adds color and flavor.

steam: To cook with moist heat by boiling water, which vaporizes into steam. The steam brings heat to the food and cooks it. Unlike boiling, the food is separate from the water and only comes into direct contact with the steam.

Boil: To heat a liquid until you see large bubbles bursting on the surface.

Simmer: To heat a liquid until little bubbles form but do not burst as in boiling.

INGREDIENTS USED IN
⚘ THIS COOKBOOK ⚘

salt

Salt is an important ingredient in both sweet and savory recipes because it enhances the flavor of any food! There are many kinds of salt, with different textures, colors and sizes. However, for this book, we are using only two main salt varieties. Kosher salt has larger crystals and is mostly used in cooking, not baking. It's easy to pinch and sprinkle into dishes without adding too much and making the recipe too salty. Fine-grain salt, such as fine sea salt or table salt, is used in baking recipes because it easily dissolves and distributes throughout the dish. If you don't have kosher salt and need to substitute it with fine salt, use half the amount. For instance, if the recipe says 1 teaspoon of kosher salt, use just ½ teaspoon of table salt.

sweeteners

We use many types of ingredients to add sweetness to a recipe, including honey, maple syrup, granulated sugar and brown sugar. All of these sweeteners have different moisture levels and flavors. In some cases, they can be substituted for one another. However, to make sure your recipe comes out the right texture, only use the sweetener or substitute that's listed in the recipe you're making.

Eggs

There are many different kinds of eggs available at grocery stores. For the recipes in this book, make sure you use large-sized eggs in whatever variety (organic, brown, white, pasture-raised, etc.) you typically have at home.

oil

We use two types of oil in this book. Extra virgin olive oil adds lots of flavor to recipes. Flavorless oil, such as avocado oil, canola oil and vegetable oil, are all interchangeable and are mostly used to brown foods and in baking.

flour

Because whole wheat flour is higher in fiber, protein and nutrients, it's often the go-to flour for recipes in this book. Baked goods made with whole wheat flour have a little more of a bitter flavor and dense texture. If you only have all-purpose flour on hand or prefer a more traditional, sweet flavor, you can use all-purpose flour instead. If you can find white whole wheat flour, that's a great flour to use, since it has the same nutritional value as regular whole wheat flour but has a more similar flavor to all-purpose flour.

☘ BEFORE-YOU-COOK CHECKLIST ☘

Stop! Before you cook, go through this checklist:

☑ *Permission Granted?* I know it's annoying, but make sure an adult knows you are cooking and is okay with the recipe you've chosen.

☑ *Read, Read, Read!* The key to cooking like a rock star? Make sure you read the recipe all the way through at least once before you start!

☑ *Ingredient Check!* Make sure you look at the ingredient list and get everything out on the counter and ready to go.

☑ *Tool Check!* You don't want to be digging through drawers to find a spatula in the middle of a recipe, so make sure you get out all the equipment you'll need.

☑ *Scrub a Dub:* Wash those hands!

☑ *Prepped and Ready!* The fancy chef phrase "mise en place" means getting all the ingredients chopped, measured and prepared before you cook. Doing this will make the actual cooking part so much easier.

☑ *You've Got This!* Take a deep breath, remember to have fun and get cooking!

FIVE-MINUTE SUPERSTAR SNACKS

Starving when you get home from school? Want an exciting snack that you can make all on your own? This chapter is full of quick bites you can whip up in no time! Whether you're craving something sweet, salty, crunchy, or all of the above, you can find exactly what you want to fill you up and power you through the rest of the day. Many of these snacks are designed to make one serving, but you can easily multiply the recipe to share with friends or siblings.

MONSTER COOKIE ENERGY BALLS

Level 1: Easy-Peasy
Makes 10 balls

Cookies without the oven? Yes, please! When you want something FAST but not boring, these energy balls are a MUST. Chock full of oats, nuts, seeds, raisins and chocolate, these LOADED cookie bites are perfect for lunch, an after-school snack or anytime! Plus, you can totally customize them with whatever mix-ins you enjoy.

Get Ready!

You need a large bowl, a big spoon or rubber spatula, a small cookie scoop or spoon and measuring cups and spoons.

Get Set!

½ cup + 2 tbsp (161 g) creamy natural peanut butter or any nut/seed butter, plus extra if needed

3 tbsp (45 ml) honey

1 tsp vanilla extract

½ cup (45 g) rolled oats

¼ cup (25 g) ground flax seeds or almond meal

2 tbsp (20 g) hemp seeds or chia seeds (optional)

2 tbsp (12 g) unsweetened finely shredded coconut (optional)

¼ cup (50 g) M&M's® minis candy or mini chocolate chips

¼ cup (36 g) raisins

Go!

1. In a large bowl, stir together the peanut butter, honey and vanilla.

2. Add the oats, ground flax seeds, hemp seeds and coconut (if using). Stir until all the ingredients are well combined. You can use your hands to squish everything together if the dough gets too thick to stir with a spoon.

3. Mix in the chocolate and raisins. Scoop up tablespoon-sized balls of dough and then roll them in your hands until smooth. If the dough is too dry to roll, stir in another 1 to 2 tablespoons (16 to 32 g) of peanut butter.

4. Store the balls in an airtight container in the fridge for up to 2 weeks (if they last more than a day!).

Chef Tip ◇·◇·◇·◇·◇·◇·◇·◇·◇·◇·◇·◇·◇·◇·◇·◇

Don't let honey get you into a sticky situation. Simply grease your measuring cup or spoon first with spray oil or by spreading a little oil around inside the cup with your fingers, and then watch the honey slide right out.

CHOCOLATE POWER-ME-UP SMOOTHIE

Want a snack that tastes like a chocolate milkshake? I've got you! Not only does this smoothie taste like dessert, but it has tons of good stuff to keep you energized and filled up to take on the rest of your day.

Level 1: Easy-Peasy
Makes 1 large or 2 small smoothies

Get Ready!

You need a liquid measuring cup, a blender, a small rubber spatula or spoon and dry measuring cups and spoons.

Get Set!

1 frozen banana

2 tbsp (11 g) unsweetened cocoa powder

1 cup (30 g) (or a small handful) baby spinach

1 tbsp (16 g) peanut butter, almond butter or sunflower seed butter

1 tbsp (15 ml) maple syrup or honey

1 cup (240 ml) milk (any type), plus ¼ cup (60 ml) extra if needed

Ice (optional)

Go!

1. Add all of the ingredients to the blender.

2. Make sure the lid is on tight, turn the blender on and blend until everything is smooth. If your blender is having trouble or the smoothie is too thick, add another ¼ cup (60 ml) of milk and blend again. For a thicker, creamier smoothie, add a handful of ice and blend again.

3. Pour the smoothie into one large glass or two small glasses. Enjoy!

Safety First! ◇·◇·◇·◇·◇·◇·◇·◇·◇·◇·◇·◇·◇·◇·

Since many blenders work differently, make sure a grown-up shows you exactly how to use the blender you have at home. Always tightly place the lid on the blender before you turn it on, and never open the top before you turn the power off. Also, never put your hands inside the blender container since there is a sharp blade at the bottom.

RAINBOW FRUIT SKEWERS

with Creamy Peanut Butter Dip

Level 1: Easy-Peasy
Makes 6–8 skewers and 1 cup (240 ml) dip

Taste the rainbow! Not only is this fruity snack beautiful, but the creamy, sweet dip takes the yum factor over the top! You can use whatever fruit you like or have on hand, but of course, if you can include every color of the rainbow in your snack, it's even more fun! The yogurt-based dip is something you are going to make over and over again to snack on all week long.

Get Ready!

You need a liquid measuring cup, a medium bowl, a small whisk or fork, a knife and cutting board, 6–8 small wooden skewers or paper lollipop sticks and dry measuring cups and spoons.

Get Set!

½ cup (120 ml) plain unflavored, unsweetened yogurt

¼ cup (65 g) peanut butter (or any nut/seed butter)

2 tbsp (30 ml) honey or maple syrup

¼ tsp ground cinnamon

1–2 cups (150–300 g) bite-sized pieces of fruit of your choice, such as strawberries, tangerines, pineapple, kiwis, blueberries and grapes

Go!

1. In a medium bowl, add the yogurt, peanut butter, honey and cinnamon. Whisk or stir with a fork to combine. Cover the dip with plastic wrap and refrigerate until ready to serve.

2. Place bite-sized pieces of the fruit onto skewers in whatever order you'd like. Serve the fruit skewers with the dip on the side. Enjoy!

VANILLA BERRY SHAKE

Level 1: Easy-Peasy
Makes 1 large or 2 small servings

Sweet, creamy, satisfying and bright pink! This special smoothie has a secret ingredient . . . frozen cauliflower! I know it sounds crazy, but if you trust me on this one, I think you'll be pleasantly surprised. You can't taste the cauliflower at all, but when blended, it makes the smoothie extra thick and creamy. If you are hesitant about the cauliflower, you can always add half the amount and add more once you get used to the idea of awesome veggies in your drink. Or just use banana instead.

Get Ready!

You need a liquid measuring cup and spoons, a blender and dry measuring cups and spoons.

Get Set!

1 cup (150 g) frozen mixed berries or strawberries

½ cup (75 g) frozen raspberries

½ cup (42 g) frozen riced cauliflower or ½ frozen banana

½ cup (120 ml) plain Greek yogurt

¼ tsp vanilla extract

1 tsp honey, 1 tsp extra if needed (optional)

1 cup (240 ml) milk (any type), plus ¼ cup (60 ml) extra if needed

Topping Ideas

Whipped topping

Rainbow sprinkles

Go!

1. Add the berries, cauliflower, yogurt, vanilla extract, honey (if using) and milk to a blender.

2. Place the top tightly on the blender, turn it onto high and blend until all the ingredients are blended and you have a smooth drink. If the smoothie is too thick to pour, add another ¼ cup (60 ml) of milk and blend again.

3. Use a spoon to taste the smoothie. If you want it to be sweeter, add another teaspoon of honey and blend again.

4. Pour the smoothie into glasses, and then top with the whipped topping and sprinkles if you'd like. Enjoy!

Waste Not!   ◇·◇·◇·◇·◇·◇·◇·◇·◇·◇·◇·◇·◇·◇·

Have leftover smoothie? Pour it into popsicle molds or little paper cups and freeze them to have as a treat later on!

ROCK STAR RANCH DIP ✦ ✶

Level 1: Easy-Peasy
Makes 2 cups (480 ml)

Everything's better with homemade dip! Veggies, crackers, pretzels . . . you name it! You can even dip a sandwich! Super easy to stir together, this creamy dip gets its signature savory flavor from garlic powder, onion powder and dill. Why "rockstar"? Well, think of this recipe as the rockstar version of your favorite ranch! Once you try it, you will quickly see why making it from scratch is so much better than buying a bottle from the store.

Get Ready!

You need a liquid measuring cup, a Mason jar with a lid or a bowl, a fork and measuring spoons.

Get Set!

1 cup (240 ml) plain Greek yogurt (whole milk or 2%)

1 cup (240 ml) mayonnaise

1 tbsp (15 ml) fresh lemon juice

1 tsp honey

1 tsp garlic powder

1 tsp onion powder

2 tsp (2 g) dried dill

½ tsp kosher salt

Fresh veggies, chips and/or crackers, for dipping

Go!

1. Place all of the ingredients in a Mason jar or bowl and stir together until the mixture is smooth and well combined.

2. Scoop some of the dip into a small bowl for serving. Serve the dip with your favorite crunchy veggies or other snacks for dipping.

3. To store, place the lid on the Mason jar or transfer the dip to an airtight container. Refrigerate for up to 1 week.

Chef Tip ◇·◇·◇·◇·◇·◇·◇·◇·◇·◇·◇·◇·◇·◇·◇·◇·

This recipe uses equal parts mayo and Greek yogurt. The mayo gives a traditional ranch creaminess, and the Greek yogurt adds a thick and creamy texture plus some protein. However, this recipe is pretty flexible. Use all mayo or all yogurt if you prefer, or you can use some sour cream in place of the yogurt.

TRAIL MIX POPCORN CLUSTERS

Get your salty, sweet AND crunchy on with this munch-tastic snack mix! This is like a loaded popcorn ball, but without all of the work! And what's better? YOU get to choose what goes into it! See how many flavor combinations you can make—change up the type of cereal, fruit and nuts or seeds for a completely different flavor profile. No boring snacks here!

Level 1: Easy-Peasy
Makes 8 cups (450 g)

Get Ready!

You need a rimmed baking sheet, parchment paper or aluminum foil, a small bowl, a fork and measuring cups.

Get Set!

6 cups (50 g) salted popcorn (either pre-popped bag or microwaved)

1 cup (120 g) pretzel sticks, broken into small pieces

1 cup (75 g) cereal of your choice

½ cup (54 g) sliced almonds or any nut/seed of your choice

1 cup (20 g) freeze-dried strawberries or any dried fruit of your choice

¾ cup (126 g) chocolate chips

Go!

1. Line a baking sheet with parchment paper or foil for easy cleanup.

2. Spread the popcorn into an even layer on the pan. Sprinkle the pretzel pieces, cereal, nuts and dried fruit over the popcorn.

3. Put the chocolate chips in a small bowl. To melt the chocolate in the microwave, heat for 30 seconds, and then remove the bowl with an oven mitt (it might be hot) and use a fork to stir the chocolate chips. Place the bowl back in the microwave and heat for another 30 seconds. Remove and continue to stir until the chocolate is fully melted.

4. Use a fork to drizzle half of the melted chocolate over the popcorn mix. Mix the trail mix together a little bit with the fork to expose any ingredients on the bottom of the pan, and then drizzle on the remaining chocolate.

5. Allow the chocolate to harden at room temperature, about 15 to 20 minutes, or speed up the process by sticking the pan in the fridge or freezer.

6. Once the chocolate is hard, break the trail mix up into clusters and enjoy. Store leftovers in an airtight container for 2 days.

SUPREME BANANA "DOGS"

Level 1: Easy-Peasy
Makes 1

What's more bananas than bananas as . . . HOT DOGS?! I know, I know, sounds silly. Hear me out! While you won't find these at any cookout, they are like a PB&J and a banana split combined! Use whatever jam and nut or seed butter you like (even Nutella®, cookie butter or granola butter!)—then pile on the toppings! Having it in a bun is the "icing" on the—well, you know—banana!

Get Ready!

You need a butter knife, a resealable plastic bag, clean kitchen scissors and measuring spoons.

Get Set!

1–2 tbsp (16–32 g) peanut butter or any nut/seed butter

1 whole wheat or white hot dog bun

1 banana

1 tbsp (20 g) raspberry jam

Topping Ideas

Sprinkles

Mini chocolate chips

Shredded coconut

Chopped nuts

Go!

1. Spread the peanut butter on the inside of the hot dog bun with the butter knife. Peel the banana and place it inside the bun so it looks like a hot dog.

2. Spoon the jam into a small resealable plastic bag. Make sure the bag is sealed well, and then snip off a corner of the bag with scissors. Squeeze the jam on top of your banana so it looks like ketchup.

3. Sprinkle on whatever toppings you'd like and enjoy!

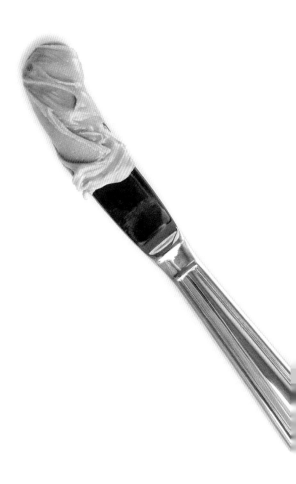

DOUBLE CHOCOLATE MUG CAKE

Level 1: Easy-Peasy
Makes 1 mug cake

Warm, gooey chocolate cake that's ready in less than 5 minutes?! Yes, it's true! No boxed cake mix here. Just a few simple ingredients you probably already have around the house, and a few minutes is all that stands between you and mug cake madness. Fast and easy at its chocolaty best!

Get Ready!

You need a liquid measuring cup, a large microwave-safe mug, a fork and measuring spoons.

Get Set!

Oil spray

¼ cup (31 g) whole wheat or all-purpose flour

2 tbsp (11 g) unsweetened cocoa powder

2 tbsp (30 g) granulated sugar

¼ tsp baking powder

⅛ tsp salt

¼ cup (60 ml) milk (any type)

1 tbsp (15 ml) vegetable oil or melted butter

1 tbsp (11 g) chocolate chips

Go!

1. Grease your mug with some oil spray.

2. Add the flour, cocoa powder, sugar, baking powder and salt to the mug and stir with a fork.

3. Stir in the milk and oil until no dry flour remains. Scrape the bottom and the side of your mug to make sure nothing is stuck.

4. Sprinkle the chocolate chips on top of the batter. Place your mug in the microwave and cook for 1 minute.

5. Use an oven mitt or towel to remove the mug, and check if the batter is set. If there is still some wet batter on the top, cook for another 15 seconds. Carefully remove the mug from the microwave, and let it sit on the counter for 1 minute to cool a bit. Dig in while it's still warm!

SPARKLING RASPBERRY WATERMELON LEMONADE

Drinks at home don't have to be boring! Why not level up basic lemonade with some bubbles?! Not only that, but bump up the flavor with some sweet fruit! This is not your typical lemonade-stand flavor. Make a double batch when your friends come over! Or just some for yourself when you're craving something bubble-licious!

Level 1: Easy-Peasy
Makes 1 large or 2 small drinks

Get Ready!

You need a liquid measuring cup, a large bowl, a potato masher, a small strainer or slotted spoon and dry measuring cups and spoons.

Get Set!

½ cup (62 g) fresh or frozen raspberries (defrost if frozen)

1 cup (152 g) diced watermelon

2 tbsp (30 ml) fresh lemon juice

1 tbsp (15 g) granulated sugar or 1 tbsp (15 ml) honey

1 cup (240 ml) sparkling water, unflavored seltzer or regular water

Ice, for serving

Go!

1. In a large bowl, add the raspberries, watermelon, lemon juice and sugar.

2. Use a potato masher to squish the fruit to get as much juice out as possible. You want to use those muscles, but don't bang the masher down too quickly or the juices will splash out of the bowl.

3. Once the fruit is smashed as much as possible, place a small strainer or slotted spoon over a liquid measuring cup, and carefully pour the fruit over the strainer so the juice drains into the measuring cup. It's okay if little pieces of fruit get into the juice.

4. Pour the strained juice into a glass or divide it into two smaller glasses for two servings. Add some ice, and then fill the glass the rest of the way with the sparkling water.

5. Stick a straw in the glass, and then use it to stir the drink. Ah, so refreshing!

Mix It Up! ◇·◇·◇·◇·◇·◇·◇·◇·◇·◇·◇·◇·◇·◇·

Lots of different fruits (fresh or frozen) work well in this yummy drink! Use blueberries, blackberries or strawberries in place of the raspberries. Instead of watermelon, use ripe peaches or mango. If you have trouble mashing up the fruit, just give it a buzz in the blender to get all that good juice out before straining.

PIZZA GRILLED CHEESE, PLEASE!

Pizza AND grilled cheese? YES! This snack combines two of our favorite things! We like cooking it in a waffle maker or sandwich press, but you can also easily make it in a skillet on the stove like a traditional grilled cheese. Get creative and fill your sandwich with whatever pizza toppings you enjoy, like cooked sausage, bacon and any veggies you may like.

Level 2: Totally Doable
Makes 1 serving

Get Ready!

Grab a cutting board; a spoon; a waffle maker, panini press or nonstick skillet; a pair of tongs or a spatula; a butter knife and measuring cups and spoons.

Get Set!

2 slices whole wheat bread

2 tbsp (30 ml) marinara or pizza sauce

½ cup (56 g) shredded mozzarella cheese

4 slices pepperoni

3–4 leaves baby spinach (optional)

Oil spray

Go!

1. Place the bread on a cutting board. Spread 1 tablespoon (15 ml) of marinara sauce in the center of each piece of bread, leaving a small border of plain bread around the edges.

2. Place half of the cheese on one slice of bread, and then top with the pepperoni slices and the spinach (if using). Add the remaining cheese on top, and then place the other slice of bread over the cheese, sauce facing down. Gently press the sandwich down to help everything stay inside.

3. To cook in the waffle maker or panini press, preheat the waffle maker/panini press. Once hot, spray the inside with oil, and then add the sandwich and press down. Cook for 2 to 3 minutes, or until the bread is golden brown and the cheese is melted. Carefully remove the sandwich to a plate with tongs or a spatula.

4. To cook on the stove, spray a small nonstick skillet with oil, and then place over medium heat. Once the pan is hot, place the sandwich in the center of the pan and cook for 2 to 3 minutes, or until golden brown. Use a spatula to carefully flip the sandwich and cook for 2 minutes, or until the other side is golden brown. Transfer the sandwich to a plate.

5. Once the sandwich is cool enough to handle, cut it in half with a butter knife and enjoy!

SMASHED GUACAMOLE
with Easy Baked Chips

Level 2: Totally Doable
Makes 2 servings

Chips and guacamole are the PERFECT anytime snack. No need to wait for Taco Tuesdays! And . . . what's better than getting to smash your food without your parents yelling about the mess! Don't have any chips on hand? No worries! You'll make your own in the oven with tortillas!

Get Ready!

Grab a cutting board, a pizza wheel or small knife, a baking pan, a spoon, a small resealable plastic bag, clean kitchen scissors, a fork and bowl (optional) and measuring spoons.

Get Set!

3 (4–6" [10–15-cm]) corn or flour tortillas

Oil spray

Kosher salt

1 large, ripe avocado, cut in half and pit removed (see the tip on page 105 for how to cut an avocado!)

1 tbsp (15 ml) lime juice (from ½ lime)

1 tbsp (3 g) finely chopped onion or scallion (optional)

2 tbsp (23 g) diced tomato (optional)

Go!

1. Preheat a toaster oven or regular oven to 350°F (180°C).

2. Lay the tortillas out on a cutting board and spray both sides of each tortilla with oil. Take a big pinch of salt and sprinkle it over the tortillas.

3. Stack the tortillas into a pile, and then use a pizza wheel or small knife to carefully cut the tortillas into wedges. Cut the stack in half and then the halves in half again to get 4 wedges from each tortilla. If you want the chips to be smaller, you can cut each of them in half again.

4. Spread the tortilla wedges out on a baking pan so they are overlapping as little as possible. Use oven mitts to carefully transfer the pan to the oven or ask a grown-up for help. Bake for 10 minutes, or until the chips are golden brown, checking on them during the last few minutes of baking to make sure they don't burn. Allow the chips to fully cool on the pan.

5. To make the smashed guacamole, scoop the flesh from the avocado into a small resealable plastic bag. Add the lime juice and ¼ teaspoon of kosher salt. Make sure to seal the top of the bag really well, removing any air inside the bag. Use your hands to mash the avocado.

6. Once the avocado is well smashed and mashed, open the bag and mix in the onion and/or tomato (if using). With the bag sealed, cut a corner off the end of the bag and squeeze the guacamole onto your chips. (You can also make the guacamole in a bowl and mash everything together with a fork.)

CARAMEL APPLE "NACHOS"

Level 2: Totally Doable
Makes 1 serving

Nachos . . . BUT apples are the chips! This snack is sweet, satisfying and SO much fun. The quick caramel sauce can also be used as a dip if you don't feel like drizzling it over the apples. The best part about making apple nachos? You can go crazy with the toppings!!

Get Ready!

Grab a small bowl, a spoon, a cutting board, a knife or apple slicer and measuring spoons.

Get Set!

2 tbsp (32 g) natural almond butter

1 tbsp (15 ml) maple syrup or 1 tbsp (14 g) brown sugar

Tiny pinch of salt

Tiny pinch of cinnamon

¼ tsp vanilla extract

1 tsp hot water, or more as needed

1 large apple, such as Honeycrisp

Topping Ideas

Mini chocolate chips

Granola

Shredded coconut

Chopped nuts

Sprinkles

Go!

1. In a small bowl, stir together the almond butter and maple syrup. Stir in the salt, cinnamon and vanilla. Add the hot water so the almond butter is warm and can easily drizzle off a spoon. If the mixture is too thick to drizzle, add a little bit more water.

2. Cut the apple into 4 wedges and cut out the core from each wedge (or use an apple slicer). Ask a grown-up for help if you need it. Cut each wedge into 3 or 4 thin slices or chop into bite-sized pieces if that's easier. Fan the apple slices out on a plate.

3. Drizzle the apples with the caramel sauce, and then sprinkle on whatever toppings you choose. Enjoy!

CRISPY BEAN AND CHEESE TAQUITOS

You're gonna want to take a pic of the epic "cheese pull" when you bite into these babies! Taquitos are like crunchy, rolled-up quesadillas. If you want, instead of beans, fill the tortillas with shredded chicken, sliced turkey, veggies—whatever you have in the fridge. Dip your cute little roll-ups in extra salsa or guacamole and you've got a seriously tasty snack or quick lunch!

Level 2: Totally Doable
Makes 4

Get Ready!

Grab an air fryer or a baking sheet, parchment paper (optional), a small bowl, a fork, a microwave-safe plate, a cutting board, tongs and measuring cups and spoons.

Get Set!

½ cup (86 g) drained and rinsed canned black beans

¼ tsp kosher salt

⅛ tsp ground cumin

⅛ tsp mild chili powder

1 tbsp (15 g) whipped cream cheese or softened regular cream cheese

1 tbsp (15 ml) jarred salsa, plus more for serving

4 small corn or flour tortillas

Oil spray

⅓ cup (37 g) shredded Mexican blend or Cheddar cheese

Go!

1. You can use an air fryer, toaster oven or regular oven for this recipe. If using an oven, preheat it to 425°F (220°C), and if using, place a piece of parchment paper on a baking sheet or air fryer basket for easy cleanup.

2. In a small bowl, add the beans, salt, cumin, chili powder, cream cheese and salsa. Use the back of a fork to roughly mash everything together.

3. Place the tortillas on a microwave-safe plate, and heat them in the microwave for 30 seconds so they are pliable and easy to roll up.

4. Place one tortilla onto a cutting board and spray it with oil. Flip the tortilla so the oiled side is facing down. Spoon a heaping spoonful of the bean mixture across the tortilla, and then top with a heaping tablespoon (7 g) of the shredded cheese.

5. Tightly roll the tortilla up, and then place it onto your air fryer basket or baking sheet with the seam facing down. Repeat with the remaining tortillas and filling.

6. For the air fryer, cook at 400°F (200°C) for 6 to 8 minutes, or until the edges of the tortillas are golden brown. For the toaster oven or oven, bake for 6 to 8 minutes, or until the edges of the tortillas are golden brown. A little of the filling might leak out the sides of the tortillas while baking—that's okay!

7. Use tongs to carefully transfer the taquitos to a plate, and let them cool for 3 to 5 minutes. Serve the taquitos warm with salsa for dipping.

BREAKFASTS OF CHAMPIONS

They say breakfast is the most important meal of the day, but it can also be the most FUN! Sweet, savory or a combo of the two—these breakfast recipes will let you get creative in the kitchen while also teaching you essential cooking skills you'll use for years to come. School-day mornings can be super busy, so make one of these breakfasts on the weekend to have in the fridge waiting to fuel you up all week.

SUPERHERO SMOOTHIE BOWLS

Level 1: Easy-Peasy
Makes 2 bowls

This bright and fruity smoothie will pump you full of energy and let you take on the day like a superhero. Smoothie bowls are thick enough to eat with a spoon, like ice cream! Plus, they are so fun to customize with your favorite toppings. Pile the toppings on or get creative and make your edible art for breakfast! Either way, your friends will be lining up to put in their smoothie bowl orders.

Get Ready!

Grab a liquid measuring cup, a high-speed blender, a spoon, a knife and cutting board (if cutting fruit as toppings) and dry measuring cups.

Get Set!

1–2 cups (30–60 g) baby spinach or chopped kale

1 frozen banana or 1 cup (150 g) frozen mango chunks

½ cup (83 g) frozen pineapple

½ cup (120 ml) vanilla or plain Greek yogurt

½ cup (120 ml) coconut water or milk (any type)

Topping Ideas

Sliced banana

Berries

Granola

Chopped nuts

Go!

1. Place all of the smoothie ingredients in the blender in the order they are listed. Make sure the lid is on tight, and then switch your blender on. Blend until smooth and thick. If your ingredients are having trouble blending, make sure to turn the blender off, and then stir everything up with a spoon and scrape down the sides. Blend again. You want to avoid adding more liquid, if possible, or the smoothie will not be thick enough.

2. Divide the smoothie between two bowls, and then smooth out the tops with the back of a spoon.

3. Add toppings of your choice and enjoy right away.

Mix It Up!

Here are some other smoothie bowl combos to try.

» Blueberry Muffin: Replace the frozen pineapple with 1 cup (148 g) of frozen blueberries and add a sprinkle of cinnamon and a spoonful of almond butter.

» Chocolate Cherry: Replace the frozen pineapple with 1 cup (154 g) of frozen cherries and add 1 tablespoon (5 g) of cocoa powder.

BERRY BREAKFAST ICE POPS

Level 1: Easy-Peasy
Makes 8 to 10 large ice pops

I give you full permission to eat ice pops for breakfast! For real? Absolutely! Because these frozen treats are a delicious combo of vanilla yogurt, sweet berries and crunchy granola, you can enjoy them at any time of the day. They are so good you might need to stick them in the back of the freezer to hide them from everyone else!

Get Ready!

You need a large liquid measuring cup, clean kitchen scissors, a spoon, 8 to 10 ice pop molds (and wooden sticks if your mold doesn't come with sticks) and dry measuring cups and spoons.

Get Set!

1 (10-oz [283-g]) bag frozen mixed berries

2 tbsp (30 ml) maple syrup or honey

1 tbsp (10 g) chia seeds (optional)

2 cups (480 ml) vanilla yogurt (preferably whole milk)

½ cup (60 g) granola

Go!

1. Let your frozen berries partially defrost by leaving the bag on the counter for 1 hour, or speed up the process by putting the berries into a liquid measuring cup or bowl and heating them in the microwave for 1 minute.

2. Add the berries to a liquid measuring cup or bowl, if they aren't already in one. Use clean kitchen scissors to snip the larger berries, like any strawberries, into little pieces. Stir in the maple syrup and chia seeds (if using). Set aside for 10 minutes to allow the chia seeds to absorb some of the berries' juices. If you aren't using chia seeds, you can just use the berries right away.

3. Layer the yogurt, berry mixture and the granola in your molds by doing 1 tablespoon (10 g) of berries, 1 tablespoon (15 ml) of yogurt and about 2 teaspoons (15 g) of granola, and then repeating that process one more time. Between layers, gently tap each mold on the counter to prevent gaps and air bubbles between the layers.

4. Place the sticks or tops on your pops, and then place in the freezer for at least 6 hours, until fully frozen. Run a mold under warm water so you can easily pull the pop out.

Chef Tip ⊙⊙⊙⊙⊙ ⊙⊙⊙⊙⊙⊙⊙⊙⊙ ⊙⊙⊙⊙⊙⊙⊙

Don't have an ice pop mold? You can layer the ingredients in small paper cups, freeze for 1 hour, and then stick in an ice pop stick. Freeze until solid, and then tear away the paper and enjoy!

GIANT BAKED PANCAKE

Level 2: Totally Doable
Makes 1 large pancake, 8 servings

Pancakes for GIANTS? No, that's silly! But this extra-large baked breakfast will feed many hungry bellies! How cool is it that you can make pancakes for the whole family without standing at the stove? Plus, any leftovers will be waiting for you in the fridge for breakfast all week. Stir up the simple pancake batter, spread it into a baking pan, and then top it however you'd like! Divide it into sections, and try out different flavor combinations. Get artsy and create a picture or pattern with your toppings. There's no limit to how you can make this pancake your own masterpiece.

Get Ready!

Grab a liquid measuring cup, a rimmed 18 x 13-inch (46 x 33-cm) baking sheet, parchment paper or foil, a knife and cutting board, a large bowl, a whisk, a medium bowl, a rubber spatula and dry measuring cups and spoons.

Get Set!

Oil spray

1 banana

6 large strawberries

4 large eggs

½ cup (120 ml) unsweetened applesauce or 1 mashed overripe banana

¼ cup (60 ml) vegetable oil

⅓ cup (80 ml) maple syrup, plus extra for serving

2 tsp (10 ml) vanilla extract

1 cup (240 ml) milk (any type)

3 cups (360 g) white whole wheat flour, all-purpose flour or a mix

1 tbsp (14 g) baking powder

1 tsp cinnamon

¼ tsp salt

Additional toppings of your choice, such as blueberries, rainbow sprinkles and/or mini chocolate chips

Go!

1. Preheat the oven to 400°F (200°C). Grease a rimmed, 18 x 13-inch (46 x 33-cm) baking sheet lightly with oil spray. Put a sheet of parchment paper or aluminum foil on the bottom of the pan for easy cleanup.

2. Peel the banana, and then slice it into thin rounds. Cut the green tops off the strawberries and place them cut side down on the cutting board. Slice them into triangles. Set the fruit aside for later.

3. In a large bowl, add the eggs, applesauce, oil, maple syrup, vanilla and milk. Use a whisk to mix everything together until well combined.

4. In a medium bowl, add the flour, baking powder, cinnamon and salt. Use a whisk to stir until all the ingredients are well combined.

5. Dump the bowl of dry ingredients into the wet ingredients and stir with a rubber spatula until everything is combined and there are no more streaks of dry flour. Pour the batter onto the baking sheet and use the rubber spatula to spread it into an even layer.

6. Decorate the top of the pancake batter however you'd like with the fruit, sprinkles and chocolate chips.

7. Use oven mitts to carefully place the baking sheet in the oven. Ask an adult for help, if needed. Set a timer for 10 minutes. When the time is up, check to make sure the edges of the pancake are lightly golden brown and the center is fully cooked. (See page 20 for more information on how to tell if it's cooked through.) If the pancake still needs more time to bake, place it back in the oven and set the timer for 2 minutes.

8. Allow it to cool for 5 to 10 minutes, and then slice into squares. Drizzle the top with extra maple syrup, if you'd like.

FIESTA BREAKFAST QUESADILLAS

Level 2: Totally Doable
Makes 2 quesadillas

This breakfast is easy enough to make before school, and it's so yummy you'll want to make it every day of the week! Do you have any favorite omelet mix-ins, like spinach, tomatoes, bacon or ham? You can totally add any of these into the eggs. Adding a little salsa to the eggs is an easy way to add tons of flavor to this dish. However, if you like to keep things simple, leave your eggs plain and dunk the cooked quesadillas into salsa or guacamole.

Get Ready!

Grab a liquid measuring cup, a small bowl, a fork or whisk, a large nonstick skillet, a rubber spatula, a plate, a cutting board, a pizza wheel or knife and dry measuring cups and spoons.

Get Set!

4 large eggs

¼ tsp kosher salt

⅓ cup (80 ml) jarred mild salsa, divided

Oil spray

2 large whole wheat tortillas

½ cup (57 g) shredded Mexican blend or Cheddar cheese, divided

Go!

1. Crack the eggs into a small bowl. Add the salt and 2 tablespoons (30 ml) of the salsa, and then use a fork or whisk to combine the ingredients and beat the eggs.

2. Heat the skillet over medium heat. Spray it with oil, and then add the egg mixture. Use a rubber spatula to stir the eggs around in the pan until they are fully cooked. The eggs should look firm with no more spots of liquid. Turn off the heat and carefully transfer the scrambled eggs to a plate.

3. Lay the tortillas out flat on a cutting board. Add 2 tablespoons (14 g) of the shredded cheese to one half of each tortilla. Divide the cooked scrambled eggs between the two quesadillas, and then sprinkle the eggs with the remaining cheese. Fold the other half of the tortilla over the filling and press down gently.

4. Wipe the pan out with a paper towel. Place the pan over medium-high heat and spray with oil. Add the assembled quesadillas to the pan and cook for 2 minutes per side, or until golden brown.

5. Turn off the heat and transfer the cooked quesadillas to the cutting board. Let them cool for 1 minute, and then cut the quesadillas into 4 wedges with a pizza wheel or knife. Serve warm with the remaining salsa on the side for dipping.

PB&J BREAKFAST COOKIES

Level 2: Totally Doable
Makes 10 large cookies

Cookies for breakfast? YES! These soft cookies taste like dessert, but they're filled with fruit, whole grains and protein to keep you full and fueled all morning. I love raspberry or strawberry jam in this recipe, but you can use any flavor you like. If you're a fan of peanut butter and jelly sandwiches, you have to bake these up ASAP!

Get Ready!

Grab a liquid measuring cup, a small bowl (for the egg), a baking sheet, parchment paper or a silicone mat, a large bowl, a whisk or fork, a rubber spatula or large spoon, a large cookie scoop if you have one, a small spoon and dry measuring cups and spoons.

Get Set!

2 very ripe bananas or 1 cup (240 ml) applesauce

⅓ cup (86 g) smooth peanut butter or any nut/seed butter

¼ cup (60 ml) maple syrup

1 large egg, cracked into a small bowl

2 tsp (10 ml) vanilla extract

½ tsp ground cinnamon

½ tsp salt

1 tsp baking powder

¾ cup (90 g) whole wheat flour

1 cup (90 g) rolled oats

2 tbsp (40 g) jam or jelly

Go!

1. Preheat the oven to 350°F (180°C). Line a baking sheet with parchment paper or a silicone baking mat.

2. In a large bowl, mash the bananas with a sturdy whisk or a fork. Once the bananas are well mashed, add the peanut butter, maple syrup, egg and vanilla. Whisk until the ingredients are well combined.

3. Add the cinnamon, salt and baking powder to the bowl and whisk to combine. Add the flour and oats, and use a rubber spatula or large spoon to stir until the flour is just mixed in.

4. Use a large cookie scoop or a ¼-cup (60-ml) measuring cup to make 10 mounds of the sticky dough on the baking sheet. Spoon ½ teaspoon of the jam onto the center of each cookie and press the top down slightly with the back of a small spoon.

5. Use oven mitts to transfer the baking sheet to the oven. Set a timer for 14 minutes, and then check if the edges of the cookies are light golden brown. If they still look pale, set a timer for 2 more minutes.

6. Use oven mitts to carefully remove the pan from the oven (or ask an adult for help). Allow the cookies to cool fully before eating or storing in an airtight container for later.

BANANA SPLIT OVERNIGHT OATS

Level 2: Totally Doable
Makes 2 servings

This breakfast tastes a little like an ice cream sundae, and it's super good for you! Have you ever had overnight oats? It's like a bowl of oatmeal, but the oats "cook" by soaking in a liquid in the fridge overnight or for at least a few hours. This overnight oats recipe, with banana, strawberry and mini chocolate chips, tastes like the ultimate ice cream sundae. What's great about overnight oats is you can make it in the evening before bed and have an awesome breakfast waiting for you in the fridge the next morning.

Get Ready!

Grab a liquid measuring cup, a medium bowl, a fork, a knife and cutting board, 2 (1-pint [480-ml]) Mason jars or other similar-sized containers and dry measuring cups and spoons.

Get Set!

1 ripe banana

1½ cups (135 g) rolled old fashioned oats

1 tbsp (10 g) chia seeds (optional)

¼ cup (65 g) almond butter (or any nut or seed butter you like)

3 tbsp (45 ml) maple syrup

1 tsp vanilla extract

Pinch of salt

2 cups (480 ml) almond milk or any milk you prefer

5–7 medium-sized (170 g) strawberries

2 tbsp (22 g) mini chocolate chips

Topping Ideas

Sliced banana

Toasted chopped nuts

Shredded coconut

Go!

1. Peel the banana and place it in a medium bowl. Use a fork to mash the banana until no large pieces remain.

2. Add the oats, chia seeds (if using), almond butter, maple syrup, vanilla and salt to the bowl. Carefully pour in the milk and stir until all the ingredients are combined. Set aside to soak.

3. Remove the green tops from the strawberries and cut them into small bite-sized pieces.

4. Layer the oat mixture and the strawberries in your jars or containers. Top the final layer of the oats with 1 tablespoon (11 g) of mini chocolate chips.

5. Place the lids or tops onto the jars and place in the refrigerator to set overnight or for at least 4 hours.

6. Enjoy straight out of the jars, as is, or add more toppings first.

OMELET BAGEL BOATS

Level 2: Totally Doable
Makes 6

This is like a bagel breakfast sandwich, BUT the bagel is stuffed with the egg and then baked! This recipe is so fun to make with a bunch of friends or family because you can set out the fillings and cheese, and then let everyone create their own special bagel boats. What will you put in yours? I'll take some tomatoes, spinach and cheese, please!

Get Ready!

Grab a baking sheet, parchment paper or aluminum foil, a serrated knife and cutting board, a spoon, a large liquid measuring cup or bowl, a fork or whisk and measuring cups and spoons.

Get Set!

3 bagels (plain or everything flavor)

6 large eggs

½ tsp kosher salt

¼ tsp ground black pepper

½ cup (57 g) shredded Cheddar cheese

Topping Ideas

Chopped spinach

Diced peppers

Diced tomatoes

Cooked and chopped bacon

Diced ham

Go!

1. Preheat the oven to 375°F (190°C). Line a baking sheet with parchment paper or aluminum foil for easy cleanup.

2. Cut your bagels in half using a serrated knife—this can be tricky, so ask a grown-up for help if you need it.

3. With a spoon, carefully scoop out most of the soft inner part of the bagel. Push down around the inside of the bagels to make the dough inside more compact and make more room. If you get a tear, just take a piece that you already removed and push it back inside the bagel to fill the hole.

4. Crack the eggs into a large liquid measuring cup or bowl. I like to use a measuring cup with a spout so it's easier to pour into the bagels. Use a fork or whisk to beat the eggs until they are very well combined. Mix in the salt and pepper.

5. Place your hollowed-out bagels on the prepared baking sheet and add your desired toppings. Slowly pour the beaten egg evenly between all the bagels. Sprinkle the tops with cheese.

6. Transfer the pan to the oven using oven mitts. Set a timer for 15 minutes and check to make sure the bagels are golden brown and the egg is set (no more liquid egg remains). If the bagels need more baking time, continue to bake for 2 more minutes.

7. Carefully remove the pan from the oven or ask a grown-up for help. Serve the bagels warm.

Waste Not!

Don't throw away your bagel insides. Besides simply snacking on them while the bagels bake, you can make them into croutons or grind them into breadcrumbs.

FLUFFY CHOCOLATE CHIP WAFFLES

Level 2: Totally Doable
Makes 8–9 waffles

Move over frozen waffles! While waffles from a box are great when you're headed out the door, this easy recipe will show you how to make the real deal. Filled with gooey chocolate chips, you'll taste the difference right away! Plus, it's super satisfying to make your family breakfast from scratch on the weekend! Of course, if you have extras, you can always try freezing these for a quick grab-n-go breakfast.

Get Ready!

Grab a small bowl (for the eggs), a medium microwave-safe bowl, a spoon, a large liquid measuring cup, a whisk, a medium bowl, a large bowl, a large spoon or rubber spatula, a waffle maker, a fork or tongs and dry measuring cups and spoons.

Get Set!

6 tbsp (85 g) unsalted butter, cut into 6 pieces, plus extra for serving

1¾ cups (420 ml) whole or 2% milk

2 tsp (10 ml) apple cider vinegar

3 cups (360 g) whole wheat flour

1 tbsp (14 g) baking powder

½ tsp ground cinnamon

¼ tsp salt

2 large eggs, cracked into a small bowl

2 tbsp (28 g) brown sugar

1 tsp vanilla extract

½ cup (84 g) mini chocolate chips

Oil spray

Maple syrup, for serving

Go!

1. To melt the butter, place it in a medium microwave-safe bowl. Place the bowl in the microwave and heat for 30 seconds. Remove the bowl using an oven mitt (it may be hot) and stir with a spoon. If the butter isn't fully melted, heat for another 15 seconds and stir again. Set the bowl aside to cool while you prepare the rest of the recipe.

2. Measure the milk into a large liquid measuring cup. Stir in the vinegar. Set aside for 5 minutes. (We are making our own buttermilk! It's normal for it to become slightly lumpy.)

3. In a medium bowl, add the flour, baking powder, cinnamon and salt. Whisk together to combine them.

4. In a large bowl, whisk together the eggs, melted butter, brown sugar and vanilla. Pour in the milk mixture and whisk again.

5. Dump the dry ingredients into the large bowl with the wet ingredients and stir with a large spoon or spatula until all the ingredients are combined. Stir in the chocolate chips.

6. Heat your waffle iron on medium-high. Once it's ready, spray both sides with oil and spoon in ⅓ cup (80 ml) of the batter. (Use more or less batter depending on the size of your waffle iron.) Cook the waffles for 5 to 6 minutes, or until golden brown. Use a fork or tongs to carefully remove the waffle from the hot iron onto a plate. Repeat with the remaining batter.

7. Serve the waffles with some extra butter and maple syrup.

Chef Tip: Measuring Brown Sugar ⊙⊙⊙⊙⊙ ⊙·

Unlike other ingredients, we always pack brown sugar into the measuring cup and spoon to get an accurate measurement. So scoop up a big cup or spoon full of brown sugar, and then press it down with the palm of your hand. Add more, press again and level off the top to make sure the measuring cup/spoon is full and even with the rim.

PUMPKIN FRENCH TOAST CUPCAKES

Level 2: Totally Doable
Makes 12 cups

Mmmmm—these sweet cups of French toast smell almost as good as they taste! Filled with pumpkin, maple and vanilla flavors, it's hard to believe that this cute, portable breakfast is made from just a few basic ingredients you probably already have at home. But that's the magic of cooking! You can serve your French toast cups with a drizzle of maple syrup or make it feel extra fancy by spreading on some maple cream cheese frosting.

Get Ready!

Grab a liquid measuring cup, a muffin tin, paper liners, a large bowl, a whisk, a spoon, a small bowl (optional) and dry measuring cups and spoons.

Get Set!

For the French Toast

8–10 slices whole grain bread or ½ large loaf challah bread

4 large eggs

¾ cup (180 ml) milk (any type)

¾ cup (184 g) canned pumpkin purée

¼ cup (60 ml) maple syrup, plus more for serving

1½ tsp (4 g) pumpkin pie spice or cinnamon

2 tsp (10 ml) vanilla extract

Pinch of salt

For the Frosting (optional)

4 oz (113 g) whipped cream cheese

2 tbsp (30 ml) maple syrup

¼ tsp vanilla extract

Go!

1. Preheat the oven to 350°F (180°C). Line the muffin tin with paper liners.

2. Cut or rip the bread into small cubes or pieces. You should have about 4 heaping cups (200 g) of bread pieces. Set aside.

3. Crack the eggs into a large bowl. Whisk in the milk, pumpkin purée, maple syrup, pumpkin pie spice, vanilla and salt. Add the bread and stir to coat. Allow the bread to soak up the egg mixture for 5 to 10 minutes, stirring occasionally.

4. Spoon the bread and custard (that's the egg-milk mixture) into the lined cups, filling them to the top. If there is any extra custard mixture left in the bowl, spoon it over the cups evenly.

5. Use oven mitts to carefully transfer the muffin pan to the oven. Set a timer for 25 minutes, and then check if the French toast cups are puffed and golden brown around the edges. If not, continue to bake for another 5 minutes. Use oven mitts to carefully remove the pan from the oven or ask a grown-up for help.

6. If you choose to make the frosting, stir the cream cheese, maple syrup and vanilla together in a small bowl. Serve the French toast cups warm with the frosting to spread on top or additional maple syrup to drizzle on top.

7. Unfrosted, baked cupcakes can be stored in the fridge for 4 to 5 days and reheated in the microwave for 1 minute before enjoying.

BANANA BREAD POWER BARS

Level 2: Totally Doable
Makes 8 bars

This super yummy banana bread is fun to make and easy to take a piece on the go! Bake up these sweet, power-packed bars, and then pop one in a lunch bag or grab for an after-school snack. Loaded with energizing seeds and filling oats, these bars will keep you going for hours. Banana power to the max!

Get Ready!

Grab a liquid measuring cup, a 9 x 9-inch (23 x 23-cm) baking dish or cake pan, parchment paper or aluminum foil, clean kitchen scissors, a large bowl, a whisk or potato masher, a large spoon or rubber spatula, a knife and cutting board and dry measuring cups and spoons.

Get Set!

Oil spray

3 medium-sized overripe bananas

¼ cup (60 ml) vegetable, canola or avocado oil

¼ cup (60 ml) maple syrup or honey

1 tsp vanilla extract

½ tsp cinnamon

¼ tsp salt

1 tsp baking powder

½ tsp baking soda

¼ cup (25 g) ground flax seeds

¼ cup (41 g) hemp seeds or chia seeds

2 cups (180 g) quick cooking rolled oats

2 tbsp (22 g) mini chocolate chips (optional)

Go!

1. Preheat the oven to 350°F (180°C). Grease a square 9 x 9-inch (23 x 23-cm) baking dish with oil spray. Cut a piece of parchment paper so it is the same width as the pan. Keep it long enough to go all the way up two sides of the pan. This creates a "sling" so you can use the long edges to pull the banana bread out of the pan after it has baked.

2. Peel the bananas and add them to a large bowl. Mash the bananas with a whisk or a potato masher. Whisk in the oil, syrup, vanilla, cinnamon, salt, baking powder and baking soda.

3. Using a spoon or rubber spatula, stir in the flax seeds, hemp seeds and oats until everything is combined.

4. Pour the batter into the prepared pan and spread it out evenly. Sprinkle the chocolate chips over the top (if using).

5. Use oven mitts to transfer the pan to the oven. Set a timer for 20 minutes and bake until golden brown around the edges. If the top still looks wet and the edges aren't lightly browned, continue baking for another 5 minutes. Carefully remove the pan from the oven with oven mitts or ask a grown-up for help.

6. Allow the banana bread to fully cool in the pan, and then use the edges of the parchment paper to lift the banana bread out of the pan, and transfer the whole thing to a cutting board. Cut the banana bread into 8 bars by cutting in half one way then into fourths the other way. Individually wrap the bars in plastic wrap or place them in an airtight container in the fridge for up to 1 week. You can also wrap and freeze the bars for up to 2 months.

Chef Tip: It's Bananas! ◎◎◎◎◎ ◎◎◎◎◎◎◎◎

Brown, spotty, overripe bananas are extra sweet, lower in starch and full of moisture, which make them perfect for using in baked treats! Bananas that are still all yellow (no brown spots) aren't quite sweet enough yet, so leave them to ripen a few more days.

SUNNY-SIDE UP BREAKFAST PIZZAS

Level 2: Totally Doable
Makes 4 individual-sized pizzas

Pizza for breakfast! It's so exciting and beyond delicious!! Store-bought flatbreads are an easy pizza hack—just pull them out of the package and top and bake. Know what's even more awesome about this dish? You crack an egg right on top and bake to your liking. It's a complete breakfast in pizza form! Plus, this egg-cellect meal is totally customizable: Add bacon or top your pizzas with whatever veggies, meats or cheese you love.

Get Ready!

Grab a sheet pan, parchment paper or aluminum foil, a small bowl, clean kitchen scissors, a spatula, a cutting board, pizza wheel or large knife and measuring cups.

Get Set!

4 whole wheat or white naan flatbreads

1 cup (112 g) shredded mozzarella cheese

1 cup (113 g) shredded Cheddar cheese

4 large eggs

Salt and pepper, to taste

4 strips cooked bacon or turkey bacon

Fresh chives, for garnish

Go!

1. Preheat the oven to 425°F (220°C). Line a sheet pan with parchment paper or foil.

2. Place the flatbreads on the baking sheet. Divide the cheeses between the breads, using ¼ cup (28 g) of each kind of cheese per bread. Spread the cheese out, but leave a circle in the center empty for the egg. It should look like the cheese is a nest for the egg. This will also help to keep the egg white from spilling off the side of the bread.

3. Crack 1 egg into a small bowl, trying not to break the yolk. Pour the egg from the bowl into the center spot on one of the flatbreads. Repeat with the remaining eggs and flatbreads. Sprinkle each egg with a small pinch of salt and pepper.

4. Use clean kitchen scissors or your fingers to break up the bacon, and sprinkle it over the cheese on each flatbread.

5. Use oven mitts to carefully transfer the baking pan to the oven or ask a grown-up for help. Bake for 10 minutes, or until the cheese is golden brown and the egg whites are cooked through (no longer transparent) but the yolks are still soft. If you like your eggs without a runny yolk, cook for another 2 minutes.

6. Use the scissors to snip some fresh chives over the top of the pizzas. Allow the pizzas to cool a little on the pan, and then use a spatula to transfer them to a cutting board, and use a pizza wheel or knife to cut into slices. Enjoy warm.

APPLE CINNAMON STREUSEL MUFFINS

Level 3: Challenge Accepted!
Makes 12 muffins

Your friends and family won't believe these muffins are homemade and not from a bakery! The sweet crumble topping and cinnamon apples make the muffins extra special without too much effort. If you don't feel like chopping the apple, you can use a box grater to shred up the apple instead.

Get Ready!

Grab a liquid measuring cup, a small bowl (for the eggs), a muffin tin, paper liners, a small bowl, a whisk, a vegetable peeler, a knife and cutting board, 2 large bowls, a medium bowl, a large spoon or rubber spatula, a cookie scoop or spoon and dry measuring cups and spoons.

Get Set!

For the Streusel

3 tbsp (45 ml) melted unsalted butter

¼ cup (55 g) brown sugar

½ tsp ground cinnamon

Pinch of salt

½ cup (60 g) white whole wheat or all-purpose flour

For the Apples

1 large or 2 small tart, crisp apples, such as Honeycrisp or Granny Smith

¼ tsp ground cinnamon

1 tbsp (14 g) brown sugar

For the Muffin Batter

1¾ cups (210 g) white whole wheat or all-purpose flour

1½ tsp (7 g) baking powder

1 tsp ground cinnamon

½ tsp baking soda

½ tsp salt

⅓ cup (80 ml) vegetable or canola oil

½ cup (120 ml) maple syrup

2 large eggs, cracked into a small bowl

½ cup (120 ml) plain Greek yogurt

½ cup (120 ml) unsweetened applesauce

1 tsp vanilla extract

Go!

1. Preheat the oven to 375°F (190°C). Line a standard muffin tin with paper liners.

2. To make the streusel, in a small bowl, mix together the melted butter, brown sugar, cinnamon, salt and flour until the mixture looks like wet, crumbly sand. Set the streusel aside for later.

3. To prepare the apple, peel the apple, and then cut the apple into a very small dice. You can use a knife to cut around the core of the apple or ask an adult for help since that part can be tricky. Once cut, you should have 1½ to 2 cups (188 to 240 g) of diced apple. Place the apple in a large bowl and mix it with the cinnamon and brown sugar. Set aside to add to the muffin batter later.

4. To prepare the batter, in a medium bowl, add the flour, baking powder, cinnamon, baking soda and salt. Use a whisk to mix the dry ingredients together until combined.

5. In a second large bowl, whisk together the oil, syrup, eggs, yogurt, applesauce and vanilla. Add the bowl of dry ingredients and stir with a large spoon or rubber spatula. Once the flour is mostly mixed in, add the apple and stir until all the ingredients are just combined.

6. Use a cookie scoop or spoon to fill each paper muffin liner almost to the top. Sprinkle the tops of each muffin with a few good pinches of the streusel mixture.

7. Use oven mitts to carefully transfer the muffin tin to the oven. Bake for 14 to 16 minutes, or until the muffins are golden brown and a toothpick inserted into the center of a muffin comes out clean. Have an adult help you take the muffin tin out of the oven.

8. Allow the muffins to cool in the tin for 10 minutes, and then transfer them to a plate or cooling rack. Keep leftovers in a container on the counter for 2 days or in the refrigerator for 5 days.

HEADLINER LUNCH BOXES

No more boring lunches! Here are some fresh and flavorful ideas to change things up. These yummy recipes will give your body the energy it needs to crush the day and have your friends begging you to make them lunch. Even if you don't bring a lunch to school, these recipes are great to have at home for easy, delicious meals any time of day. Some of these recipes are great to make ahead on the weekend and others are perfect for packing up the night before.
Either way, you've got lunch covered!

BUILD-YOUR-OWN MINI TACOS

Level 1: Easy-Peasy
Makes 1 lunch

Assembling your own tacos at lunchtime is so fun! If you don't want to use beans in this recipe, you can use shredded cooked chicken or any taco-style meat you might have left over from a taco night dinner. Using a bento box–style container is great for packing up all the taco toppings separately.

Get Ready!

You need a knife and cutting board (to dice tomatoes), a 2" (5-cm)-round cookie cutter or similar-sized glass with a thin rim, a small bowl, a spoon and measuring cups and spoons.

Get Set!

1 large flour tortilla or 3 mini flour tortillas

1 cup (172 g) drained and rinsed canned black or pinto beans

2 tbsp (30 ml) jarred mild salsa

½ tsp mild chili powder

¼ tsp kosher salt

½ cup (57 g) shredded Cheddar or Monterey Jack cheese

¼ cup (45 g) sliced grape/cherry tomatoes

¼ cup (14 g) shredded lettuce

Topping Ideas

Sour cream

Guacamole

Sliced olives

Salsa

Go!

1. If you have a large tortilla, use a large, round cookie cutter or the rim of a glass to cut the tortilla into 3 smaller 2-inch (5-cm) circles. These will be your mini taco shells.

2. In a small bowl, add the beans, salsa, chili powder and salt. Mix to combine all the ingredients.

3. Pack the tortilla, beans, cheese, tomato, lettuce and any additional toppings in a lunch box or bento box–style container and include a spoon for assembly. Eat right away or store in the fridge until you're ready to pack your lunch. Pack with an ice pack until lunchtime. When ready to eat, take a tortilla and spoon on some beans and top with cheese, tomatoes and lettuce and any other toppings you packed.

STELLAR SANDWICH POCKETS

Level 1: Easy-Peasy
Makes 1 lunch

Want to step up your sandwich game? Here's a fun idea that doesn't take much effort at all! These crustless, portable pockets have endless possibilities. Just cut your favorite soft sandwich bread into a circle, add a filling, and fold into a mini pocket sandwich. It's like the homemade version of those popular frozen crustless PB&J sandwiches, but these homemade ones are more fun to make and eat! Mix and match from the fillings in this recipe, or create your own tasty concoction!

Get Ready!

Grab a 5" (13-cm) round cookie or biscuit cutter or similar-sized glass with a thin rim (or other large cookie cutter shape such as a heart or star), a butter knife, fork and measuring spoons.

Get Set!

4 slices soft sandwich bread

Filling of your choice (see ideas below)

Sunflower Seed Butter and Raspberry

2 tbsp (32 g) sunflower seed butter or any nut butter

8 fresh raspberries or jam

Egg and Avo

1 hard-boiled egg, peeled

¼ avocado (see the tip on page 105 for how to cut an avocado!)

½ tsp lemon juice

Salt and pepper

Hummus and Veggie

2 tbsp (28 g) hummus

2 tbsp (14 g) grated carrot

2 tbsp (18 g) chopped cucumber or bell pepper

Go!

1. Using one of the suggested tools in the Get Ready! section, cut each slice of bread into the biggest circle you can cut out without going over the crust. Save the scraps for another use (see tip below).

2. Flatten out the bread by pressing all over the circle with your fingertips. Place the filling of your choice in the center of the circle, leaving a small, clear border around the circle.

3. Now it's time to add your filling choice!

For the sunflower seed butter and raspberry filling, spread ½ tablespoon (8 g) of sunflower seed butter on each piece of bread and top with 2 raspberries each.

For the egg and avo filling, mash all the ingredients together in a small bowl and season with salt and pepper to taste. Top each piece of bread with ½ tablespoon (5 g) of the egg mash, evenly dividing the mixture between the 4 pieces.

For the hummus and veggie filling, spread each piece of bread with ½ tablespoon (7 g) of the hummus and ½ tablespoon (8 g) of each of the veggies.

4. To close the pockets, fold the bread circle in half, and then pinch the outer edges together to seal the bread into a half circle. Press the tines of a fork around the edge to further seal and decorate your sandwich pocket. Eat right away or store in the fridge until you're ready to pack your lunch box. Pack with an ice pack until lunchtime.

Waste Not! ◇·◇·◇·◇·◇·◇·◇·◇·◇·◇·◇·◇·◇·◇·◇

No need to throw those bread crusts away! Stick them in a bag and throw them in the freezer. Once you have a full bag, buzz them in a food processor to make breadcrumbs. You can also rip them up and toast them with some oil to make croutons for a salad, or use them in the Pumpkin French Toast Cupcakes recipe on page 70.

WAFFLE-WICH ON A STICK

Level 1: Easy-Peasy
Makes 1 lunch

While we all love breakfast for dinner, how about breakfast for LUNCH?! This sweet and savory combo is the perfect answer to the midday munchies. Because we use the cutest mini waffles (or pancakes!) from the freezer section of your grocery store, this lunch is super quick and easy. Plus, bright, fresh berries make it loaded with fruit flavor. The skewers add an extra fun touch, but if you're short on time, just place the lil' sammies in a container with the fruit on the side.

Get Ready!

Grab a knife and cutting board, a butter knife, 2 small wooden skewers and measuring cups and spoons.

Get Set!

8 mini frozen waffles, toasted

2 tbsp (29 g) cream cheese or any nut/seed butter

2 tbsp (40 g) strawberry or raspberry jam

¼ cup (37 g) blueberries

6 large strawberries, cut into halves or quarters

Go!

1. Spread 4 of the mini waffles with a thin layer of cream cheese and then spread the other 4 waffles with jam.

2. Put the cream cheese and jam waffles together to make sandwiches.

3. Put the fruit and waffles on the skewers however you like, using 2 waffle sandwiches per stick.

PIZZA LUNCH BOX MUFFINS

Level 2: Totally Doable
Makes 12 muffins

Pizza in a muffin, huh? I know muffins are usually sweet, but think of savory muffins as sandwiches in a different form. They are super delicious and easy to eat, and bonus points that they are packed with all the nutrients you need to fuel your body and brain midday. If you make the muffins on the weekend, you can enjoy a couple while they're warm from the oven (the best!), and then save the extras for yummy lunches and snacks all week! The spinach gives this lunch a nice little veggie boost, but you can leave it out or use other veggies, like chopped broccoli or bell peppers, if spinach isn't your thing.

Get Ready!

Grab a liquid measuring cup, a knife and cutting board, a muffin tin, paper liners, a large bowl, a whisk, a wooden spoon or rubber spatula, a cookie scoop (optional) and dry measuring cups and spoons.

Get Set!

2 large eggs

¼ cup (60 ml) olive oil or vegetable oil

1 cup (240 ml) milk (any type)

1 tbsp (16 g) tomato paste

¼ tsp garlic powder

1 tsp baking powder

½ tsp baking soda

¼ tsp fine salt

¼ tsp dried oregano

1½ cups (180 g) whole wheat flour

¼ cup (8 g) roughly chopped or ripped up baby spinach

⅓ cup (57 g) chopped pepperoni or mini pepperoni (optional)

1 cup (112 g) shredded mozzarella cheese, divided

Go!

1. Preheat the oven to 350°F (180°C) and line the muffin tin with 12 paper liners.

2. In a large bowl, add the eggs, oil, milk and tomato paste. Whisk to combine, and then whisk in the garlic powder, baking powder, baking soda, salt and oregano.

3. Add the flour and mix with a wooden spoon or rubber spatula until most of the flour is mixed in. Stir in the spinach, pepperoni (if using) and about half of the cheese, leaving the other half of the cheese to sprinkle on top of the muffins.

4. Use a ⅓-cup (80-ml) measuring cup or a large cookie scoop to evenly divide the muffin batter between the muffin cups, filling each one three-quarters full. Top each muffin with a pinch of the remaining cheese.

5. Using oven mitts, carefully place the muffin tin onto the center rack of your oven. Set a timer for 18 minutes, and bake until the tops of the muffins are golden brown and a toothpick or the tip of a butter knife inserted into the center of a muffin comes out clean. If there's still wet batter in the center, set a timer for 4 minutes and continue to bake. Ask an adult if you need help removing the pan from the oven.

6. Allow the muffins to cool in the pan for 5 minutes, and then carefully transfer them to a cooling rack to cool completely. Store muffins in an airtight container in the fridge for up to 5 days or in the freezer for up to 1 month.

Chef Tip: Better Batter ◇·◇·◇·◇·◇·◇·◇·◇·◇·◇

Don't overmix the batter! When stirring flour into liquid ingredients, make sure to stir only until all the white dry flour disappears, then stop. If you keep stirring, your final dish might end up tough and too chewy.

CHICKEN CAESAR SALAD KEBABS

Level 2: Totally Doable
Makes 6 skewers

Everything is more fun on a stick! This isn't your typical salad lunch since all of the components are separate, and you can choose to include what you like. Serve the kebabs with the easy, creamy homemade dressing for dipping and you have a seriously tasty lunch!

Get Ready!

Grab a liquid measuring cup, a small bowl, a whisk or fork, a knife and cutting board, 6 small wooden skewers or paper lollipop sticks and measuring spoons.

Get Set!

¼ cup (60 ml) mayonnaise or plain Greek yogurt

2 tbsp (30 ml) extra virgin olive oil

1 tbsp (15 ml) red wine vinegar or lemon juice

½ tsp garlic powder

½ tsp Dijon mustard

½ tsp Worcestershire sauce

2 tbsp (13 g) grated Parmesan cheese

Pinch of ground black pepper

4 Romaine lettuce leaves

2 slices focaccia bread or any bread

1 (6–8-oz [170–226-g]) cooked chicken breast (such as leftover cooked chicken or store-bought rotisserie chicken)

8 cherry or grape tomatoes

Go!

1. First, make the dressing! In a small bowl, whisk together the mayo, olive oil, vinegar, garlic powder, mustard, Worcestershire sauce, Parmesan cheese and pepper. Refrigerate until ready to use or pack in small containers.

2. Cut the lettuce, bread and chicken into bite-sized pieces or cubes. Cut the tomatoes in half. Place all of these ingredients onto 6 small skewers in any order you like.

3. Eat right away or pack the skewers into containers with some dressing on the side for dipping, and store in the fridge until you're ready to pack your lunch box. Pack with an ice pack until lunchtime.

Mix It Up! ◇·◇·◇·◇·◇·◇·◇·◇·◇·◇·◇·◇·◇·◇·

Create different sandwich kebab combinations. Try hard-boiled egg, cheese cubes, rolled ham or turkey, bacon, cucumber chunks and different kinds of bread.

DIY YOGURT PARFAITS

with Crunchy Maple Granola

Level 2: Totally Doable
Makes 4 cups (450 grams) granola and 1 lunch parfait

Breakfast for lunch is a favorite at my house! I kept this easy granola recipe nut-free since many schools don't allow nuts because of allergies. However, if you are making this just to have at home or you don't need the granola to be nut-free, add in any sliced or chopped nuts you like instead of all or some of the seeds. Pack the granola separately from your favorite yogurt, berries or chopped fruit so that you can assemble and enjoy your perfect parfait right at lunchtime. Round out your lunch with a hard-boiled egg or some sliced turkey and some crunchy veggies.

Get Ready!

Grab a liquid measuring cup, a baking sheet or large plate, a 10" or 12" (25- or 30-cm) skillet, a wooden spoon, a spatula and dry measuring cups and spoons.

Get Set!

For the Nut-Free Granola

3 tbsp (45 ml) coconut oil or vegetable oil

⅓ cup (80 ml) maple syrup or honey

2 cups (180 g) rolled oats

½ cup (47 g) unsweetened shredded coconut flakes

½ cup (69 g) raw pumpkin seeds

½ cup (67 g) raw sunflower seeds

Pinch of salt

¼ tsp ground cinnamon

For the Parfaits

1 cup (240 ml) vanilla Greek yogurt or any type you like

1 cup (135 g) mixed berries such as sliced strawberries, raspberries and blueberries

½ cup (60 g) nut-free granola (above) or other granola of your choice

Go!

1. Set a baking sheet or large plate next to the stove. This is where the granola will cool once it has cooked.

2. To make the granola, add the oil and maple syrup to a large skillet. Place the skillet on the stove and turn the heat to medium-high.

3. Add the oats to the pan and cook, stirring frequently, for 2 to 3 minutes, or until the oats begin to toast.

4. Add the coconut, pumpkin seeds, sunflower seeds, salt and cinnamon, and cook, stirring often, for 5 to 8 minutes, or until everything is a light golden brown. If the ingredients start to turn golden brown too quickly, turn the heat down to medium or low. This will help prevent them from burning.

5. Dump the granola onto the baking sheet or plate and use a spatula to spread it out to an even layer, and then let the granola cool completely. Once cool, you can use it to make the parfaits, or transfer it to an airtight container and store on the counter for up to 10 days.

6. To pack up the parfaits in your lunch box, place the yogurt, berries and granola in separate leak-free containers. Pack with an ice pack until lunchtime. When ready to eat, add the berries and granola on top of the yogurt and enjoy.

HAM AND CHEESE SUPER SPIRALS

Level 2: Totally Doable
Makes 12 rolls

Move over plain old sandwiches. Ham and cheese got an upgrade big time! These baked cheese-stuffed rolls are great to keep in the fridge for a hearty afterschool snack or quick dinner. To make it super easy to roll up the spirals, use a thin-crust version of canned pizza dough, which you can find in the refrigerated section of the grocery store next to the canned biscuits. But this method also works with any regular pizza dough as long as you roll it out super thin. If you don't like or eat ham, feel free to use deli turkey instead.

Get Ready!

You will need a baking sheet, parchment paper or aluminum foil, a rolling pin (optional), a spoon or pastry brush, a serrated knife and measuring cups and spoons.

Get Set!

Oil spray (optional)

1 (11-oz [311-g]) tube thin-crust pizza dough or 1 ball pizza dough

2 tbsp (30 ml) honey mustard (optional)

1 cup (30 g) baby spinach

½ lb (226 g) thin-sliced deli ham

¼ lb (113 g) sliced Cheddar cheese (8 to 10 slices)

1 tbsp (9 g) poppy seeds or sesame seeds (optional)

Go!

1. Preheat the oven to 375°F (190°C). Line a baking sheet with parchment paper or aluminum foil. If using foil, grease with oil spray.

2. Unroll the pizza dough onto a clean work surface. If you are using regular pizza dough, use a rolling pin to roll the dough out very thin into a 16 x 10-inch (41 x 25-cm) rectangle.

3. If using, spread the honey mustard evenly over the entire surface of the dough with the back of a spoon or a pastry brush.

4. Tear up the spinach with your fingers and scatter it all over the dough.

5. Lay the ham on to cover the entire surface of the dough as best you can, and then do the same thing with the sliced cheese.

6. Starting with the longer side of the dough, roll the whole thing up into a tight log. Pinch the dough together along the seam to seal the roll. If using seeds to decorate the outside of the dough, sprinkle them over the top and roll the dough around so the seeds go around the sides too.

7. Use a serrated knife to trim about a ¼ inch (6 mm) off the ends of the roll to make it even. Cut the entire log of dough into 12 equal pieces. Do this by first cutting it in half, and then cutting each half in half, and then cutting each of those 4 pieces into 3 equal pieces. Place each piece cut side up on the prepared baking sheet.

8. Use oven mitts to transfer the baking sheet to the oven. Bake for 20 minutes, or until the rolls are golden brown and the centers look cooked through. Carefully remove the pan from the oven or ask for help. Allow the rolls to cool on the pan, and eat them while warm or store in the fridge until you're ready to pack your lunch box. Pack with an ice pack until lunchtime.

RAINBOW TORTELLINI SALAD

Level 2: Totally Doable
Makes 4 servings

"Eating the rainbow" is easy and delicious when you make this colorful pasta dish! You can customize this recipe with any type of cooked or raw veggies you like or have in the fridge. We love tortellini because it's stuffed with cheesy goodness, but if you don't have it, use ½ pound (226 g) of your favorite pasta shape. Toss it with the flavorful dressing and you'll have a yummy lunch waiting for you all week.

Get Ready!

Grab a knife and cutting board, a liquid measuring cup, a large pot, a colander, a large bowl, a vegetable peeler, a box grater, a small bowl or Mason jar, a fork, a large spoon and dry measuring cups and spoons.

Get Set!

Water, for cooking the tortellini

1 (20-oz [567 g]) package refrigerated cheese tortellini

8 mini bell peppers (red, orange and yellow) or 1 large red bell pepper

3 small cucumbers

2 large carrots

1 cup (70 g) finely chopped red cabbage or shredded purple carrot

¼ cup (60 ml) extra virgin olive oil

2 tbsp (30 ml) red wine vinegar

1 tsp garlic powder

½ tsp kosher salt, plus more if needed

¼ tsp ground black pepper, plus more if needed

¼ cup (25 g) grated Parmesan cheese

Go!

1. With a grown-up's help, bring a large pot of water to a boil. Cook the tortellini according to the package instructions. Drain the pasta in a colander in the sink, and then rinse it with cold water to cool it off. Set aside.

2. Chop the peppers and cucumbers into small bite-sized pieces and add them to a large bowl. Peel the carrots and shred them on the large holes of a box grater or finely chop them. Add the carrot to the bowl of veggies, along with the cabbage.

3. In a small bowl or Mason jar, add the oil, vinegar, garlic powder, salt, pepper and Parmesan cheese. Use a fork to whisk the dressing in the bowl, or place the lid on the jar tightly and shake it up.

4. Add the cooled tortellini to the bowl with the chopped vegetables, and then pour the dressing over the top. Stir with a large spoon to coat everything in the dressing. Taste the pasta salad and add more salt and pepper if it seems like it needs more seasoning.

5. Serve right away or pack up in containers and store in the fridge for 3 to 4 days. Pack a container in your lunch box with an ice pack until lunchtime.

BARBECUE CHICKEN BISCUIT BOMBS

Level 2: Totally Doable
Makes 8

Savory barbecue chicken and melty cheese wrapped in a tender, flaky biscuit crust . . . they are da' BOMB! These little packages of deliciousness taste so good you'd never realize how easy they are to make (thanks to store-bought biscuit dough!). Use this recipe as a starting point to create your own biscuit bomb creations with different fillings like leftover meat from taco night or scrambled eggs with cheese for a breakfast-y version. YUM!

Get Ready!

Grab a liquid measuring cup, a baking sheet or air fryer, a medium bowl, a spoon, a cutting board, a fork, and dry measuring cups and spoons.

Get Set!

1 cup (125 g) cooked shredded or chopped chicken

¼ cup (18 g) finely grated carrot or chopped spinach (optional)

¼ cup (60 ml) barbecue sauce

1 can (8 pieces) biscuit dough

1 cup (113 g) shredded Cheddar cheese

Go!

1. You can use an oven or an air fryer to cook these. If using an oven, preheat it to 350°F (180°C).

2. Add the chicken, veggies (if using) and barbecue sauce to a medium bowl. Stir everything together until well mixed.

3. Open the can of biscuits following the instructions on the package. Split one biscuit in half with your fingers, and place both halves onto a cutting board or work surface. Press the dough flat with your fingertips, making each circle a little larger and an even thickness throughout.

4. Place 2 tablespoons (27 g) of the chicken mixture onto the center of one of the circles of dough. Add 1 tablespoon (7 g) of shredded cheese on top of the chicken, and then place the other circle of dough on top of that.

5. Press the outer edges of the dough down with your fingertips. Using a fork, press the ends of the fork into the dough all around the circle to seal the two sides of dough together. Push the fork into the top of the biscuit circle to make some holes—this will create a vent for hot air to escape while the biscuits are baking. Place the finished biscuit onto your baking sheet or in the air fryer basket in one layer.

6. Repeat the process above with the remaining biscuits and filling. Once your air fryer is full, leave the remaining biscuits on your work surface or a plate until ready to cook.

7. For the oven, bake the biscuits for 12 to 14 minutes, or until very golden brown and the biscuits are cooked through. For the air fryer, cook at 350°F (180°C) for 10 to 12 minutes. If using the air fryer, you will have to make these in a few batches depending on how many fit in your air fryer basket at one time.

8. Serve the biscuit bombs either fresh and warm, or let them cool to room temperature. Store in the fridge until you're ready to pack your lunch box. Pack with an ice pack until lunchtime.

DIP-TASTIC LUNCH

with Homemade Hummus

Level 2: Totally Doable
Makes 1½ cups (560 g)
of hummus

When you get tired of sandwiches, mix it up with this dip-tastic lunch! Once you realize how easy and tasty it is to make your own hummus, I know you'll want to start experimenting with dippers and hummus mix-ins. Bonus? No more boring, soggy sandwiches!

Get Ready!

Grab a liquid measuring cup, a colander, food processor or blender, a small bowl, a rubber spatula or spoon and dry measuring cups and spoons.

Get Set!

1 (15-oz [425-g]) can chickpeas, drained and rinsed

½ lemon

¼ cup (60 g) tahini (sesame paste)

1 tsp garlic powder or 1 small clove garlic

2 tbsp (30 ml) extra virgin olive oil

¼ cup (60 ml) water

¼ tsp kosher salt, or more if needed

Lunch Box Ideas

Fresh veggies

Pretzels or crackers

Apple slices

Strawberries

Sunflower seed butter

Creamy Peanut Butter Dip (page 31)

Go!

1. Add the chickpeas to a food processor or blender. Squeeze the lemon half over a small bowl to catch any seeds. Measure 1 tablespoon (15 ml) of lemon juice and add it over the chickpeas.

2. Add the tahini, garlic powder, oil, water and salt to the food processor, close the lid and press ON. Blend until the hummus is smooth and creamy, stopping and scraping down the sides of the food processor bowl as needed with a spatula or spoon.

3. Once the hummus is fully blended, give it a taste. Does it need more salt or lemon juice to taste good to you? Add a little more and blend again. Scoop the hummus into a resealable container and store in the fridge for up to a week.

4. To pack your dip-tastic lunch, add some hummus to a small container, and then pack it up in a lunch box with your favorite crunchy veggies, crackers or pretzels and some fruit with a small container of sunflower seed butter or other dip of your choice. Pack with an ice pack until you're ready to eat.

Mix It Up! New Hummus Flavors ◇·◇·◇·◇·◇·◀

» **Red Pepper:** Blend in ½ cup (70 g) of jarred roasted red peppers, drained and patted dry.

» **Everything Bagel:** Blend in 1 tablespoon (8 g) of everything bagel seasoning or 1 teaspoon of sesame seeds, 1 teaspoon of poppy seeds and ½ teaspoon of onion powder.

» **Dill Pickle:** Blend in 1 teaspoon dried dill and 2 chopped dill pickle spears.

FIVE-STAR DINNERS

These dinner recipes will teach you to cook like a master chef! Tell your family that you've got dinner covered because these meals are more delicious than anything you can order in. Did you know you can travel the world through your taste buds? Some of the recipes in this chapter are inspired by flavors and cuisines from around the globe. They are seriously tasty and fun to make, so don't be afraid to try something new. Cooking dinner on your own will give you skills you'll use for a lifetime, and more importantly, make you feel like a superstar!

ONE-POT MAC AND CHEESE WITH TREES

Level 2: Totally Doable
Makes 4 servings

Are you obsessed with creamy, cheesy pasta? Me too! Ditch the box because you won't believe how easy this mac is to make from scratch. You cook both the pasta and the sauce at the same time and in the same pot—it's like a magic trick! If you don't love broccoli, feel free to leave it out, or stir in some frozen peas when you add the cheese at the end of the recipe. American cheese makes the sauce extra creamy, but if you don't have any, you can replace it with 1 more cup (113 g) of shredded Cheddar.

Get Ready!

Grab a large liquid measuring cup, a large pot, a wooden spoon and dry measuring cups and spoons.

Get Set!

2 cups (480 ml) whole or 2% milk

1 cup (240 ml) water

½ tsp kosher salt

2 cups (128 g) elbow macaroni or small shell pasta

2 cups (182 g) frozen broccoli florets

1 cup (113 g) shredded Cheddar cheese

3 slices American cheese, ripped into pieces

Go!

1. In a large pot, add the milk, water and salt and place the pot over medium heat. Once the pot starts to bubble, stir in the pasta and turn the heat down to medium-low. Cook the pasta for 5 minutes, stirring often and making sure the pot doesn't boil over. If the liquid starts to bubble up close to the top of the pot, turn the heat down more and keep stirring.

2. After 5 minutes, stir in the broccoli and cook for 5 minutes, or until the pasta is tender.

3. Turn off the heat and add the Cheddar cheese and American cheese. Stir until the cheese is fully melted and the sauce is creamy. Serve!

Chef Tip

If using fresh broccoli for this recipe, use a small paring knife to cut small florets off of the larger head of broccoli. You want all the florets to be roughly the same size so they cook in the same amount of time.

CHICKEN FAJITA BURRITO BOWLS

◇

◇

Level 2: Totally Doable
Makes 4 servings

This mash-up of fajitas and burritos makes the BEST easy dinner! Pile the colorful peppers and chicken on rice, then top with whatever you love in your burrito. Bowl meals are so fun to make and easy for everyone to customize, but if you love tortillas, you can totally wrap everything up instead. Next time you and your family are craving burritos, tell everyone you've got dinner covered!

Get Ready!

Grab a knife and cutting board, a small bowl, a spoon, a large skillet or nonstick pan, a wooden spoon and dry measuring cups and spoons.

Get Set!

1 red bell pepper

1 orange or yellow bell pepper

½ large onion

2 tsp (6 g) garlic powder

1 tsp mild chili powder

1 tsp paprika

½ tsp ground cumin

1 tsp kosher salt

1 tbsp (15 ml) extra virgin olive oil

1 lb (454 g) ground chicken or turkey

4 cups (744 g) cooked white or brown rice

1 ripe avocado, cut into quarters and sliced

1 cup (240 ml) fresh salsa or diced tomatoes

¼ cup (4 g) fresh cilantro leaves (optional)

¼ cup (60 ml) plain Greek yogurt or sour cream

Go!

1. Cut the peppers and onion into a small dice. In a small bowl, mix together the garlic powder, chili powder, paprika, cumin and salt.

2. Heat the oil in a large skillet over medium-high heat. Add the diced peppers and onion. Cook, stirring frequently, for 2 to 3 minutes, or until the veggies begin to brown.

3. Add the ground chicken, and use a wooden spoon to break the meat up into little bits. Sprinkle the spice mixture over the meat and veggies and continue to stir for 3 to 4 minutes, or until the meat is cooked through.

4. To serve, spoon the chicken and veggies over the cooked rice and top with avocado, salsa, cilantro (if using) and a dollop of yogurt or sour cream.

Chef Tip: Cutting Avocados ⊙⊙⊙⊙⊙ ⊙⊙⊙⊙⊙

Cutting an avocado can be tricky because it's round and there's a large pit in the center. First, place the avocado down on a cutting board the long way (so the top part is facing away from you). Carefully slice down the avocado lengthwise until you hit the pit. Pick up the avocado and gently roll it around the knife so you are cutting it all the way around the center. Remove the knife, and then use both hands to twist open the avocado to separate the two halves. Cut each of those halves in half again to get four pieces. This will make it easy to remove the pit and peel away the skin.

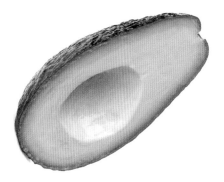

EASY-PEASY NOODLE STIR-FRY

Level 2: Totally Doable
Makes 4 servings

While takeout is great, sometimes you want to make your favorite restaurant foods at home. Packed with veggies and LOADED with flavor, this dish also comes together in only a bit more time than it takes to make a plate of pasta! Once you have the sauce ingredients, this will become your new takeout fake-out. Want extra protein? Just stir in some cooked chicken, steak or shrimp at the end.

Get Ready!

Grab a liquid measuring cup, a box grater (for the carrot), a large pot, a knife and cutting board, garlic press (optional), a wooden spoon, tongs, a large bowl, a colander (optional), a small bowl, a fork or small whisk, a large skillet or wok and dry measuring cups and spoons.

Get Set!

Water, for cooking noodles

1 bunch scallions

1 red bell pepper

2 cloves garlic

8 oz (226 g) uncooked rice noodles or whole wheat spaghetti

2 tbsp + 1 tsp (35 ml) vegetable or canola oil, divided

¼ cup (60 ml) low-sodium soy sauce

2 tbsp (30 ml) hoisin sauce or oyster sauce

1 tbsp (15 ml) rice wine vinegar

1 tbsp (15 ml) honey

1 (8-oz [226-g]) package sliced mushrooms

½ cup (73 g) snow peas or sugar snap peas

1 cup (110 g) shredded carrot

Go!

1. Fill a large pot halfway with water and set it on the stovetop over high heat to bring it to a boil.

2. While you wait for the water to boil, prepare the veggies. Trim and discard the ends off the scallions, and then thinly slice the white and green parts. Keep the sliced white parts separate from the green parts. Thinly slice the pepper. Use a garlic press or knife to mince the garlic.

3. Once the water is boiling, carefully add the noodles and stir to make sure they don't stick together. Cook according to the package directions. Once cooked, turn off the heat and use tongs to transfer the cooked noodles to a large bowl or ask a grown-up to help you drain the noodles into a colander in the sink.

4. Rinse the noodles with cold water. Drizzle the noodles with 1 teaspoon of oil and toss with the tongs to prevent the noodles from sticking together.

5. In a small bowl, stir together the soy sauce, hoisin sauce, rice vinegar and honey. Set aside.

6. Set a large skillet or wok on the stovetop over medium-high heat. Add 1 tablespoon (15 ml) of the oil. Add the white parts of the scallions and the mushrooms. Cook, stirring every minute or so, for 3 to 4 minutes, or until the veggies have started to brown. Add the remaining oil to the skillet and add the bell pepper, garlic, snow peas and shredded carrot. Cook while stirring for 2 to 3 minutes, or until the veggies have softened. If the garlic is starting to get brown, turn the heat down to medium to prevent it from burning.

7. Add the noodles to the pan and pour in the sauce. Turn the heat off and toss everything together with the tongs. Sprinkle with the sliced green part of the scallions and serve.

PRESTO! PESTO SPAGHETTI

Level 3: Challenge Accepted!
Makes 4 servings

Super green and super yummy—pesto is the best-o! Although pesto is traditionally made with all basil, we also add spinach in this recipe because it makes the sauce milder and a little sweeter. Just dump all the ingredients into a food processor and PRESTO—you've got a tasty sauce for spaghetti, other types of pasta, pizza and more!

Get Ready!

Grab a liquid measuring cup, a large pasta/soup pot, a food processor or blender, a wooden spoon, tongs, a spoon or small rubber spatula, a large bowl, a knife and cutting board, tongs, a colander (optional) and dry measuring cups and spoons.

Get Set!

Water, for cooking spaghetti

1 tbsp + ½ tsp (21 g) kosher salt, divided

1 (12-oz [340-g]) box thin spaghetti

1 small clove garlic or ½ tsp garlic powder

⅓ cup (36 g) sliced or slivered almonds or any nut or seed

2 packed cups (75 g) baby spinach

1 packed cup (30 g) fresh basil leaves, plus extra for garnish

1 tsp lemon juice

½ tsp honey (optional)

¼ cup (25 g) grated Parmesan cheese, plus more for serving

¼ cup (60 ml) extra virgin olive oil

2 cups (298 g) cherry or grape tomatoes, cut in half or quarters

8 oz (226 g) small fresh mozzarella balls or fresh mozzarella, diced (optional)

Go!

1. Fill a large pot halfway with water, and set it on the stovetop over high heat to come to a boil. Once the water is boiling, add 1 tablespoon (18 g) of the salt and carefully add the spaghetti. Stir to make sure the pasta doesn't stick together and it is all submerged in the water. Lower the heat to medium-low so the water is simmering but doesn't boil over. Cook according to the package directions.

2. To make the pesto, have a grown-up help make sure the food processor is plugged in and the metal blade is in place inside the bowl. Smash the garlic clove with the bottom of a measuring cup and remove the outer peel. Place the garlic clove, nuts, spinach, basil, lemon juice, honey (if using), cheese, olive oil and the remaining salt into the food processor. Close the lid and press the ON button. Allow the machine to blend the pesto for 20 to 30 seconds. Stop and scrape down the sides of the bowl. Process again until the pesto is creamy and well blended. It's okay if the pesto isn't completely smooth.

3. Carefully remove the food processor blade and set aside. Spoon all the pesto into the bottom of a large bowl.

4. Once the pasta is cooked, turn off the heat and use tongs to grab the pasta and transfer it to the bowl with the pesto. (Alternatively, have a grown-up help you drain the pasta into a colander in the sink, but make sure you save 1 cup [240 ml] of the pasta water first, and then add the pasta to the bowl with the pesto.)

5. Use the tongs to toss the pasta with the pesto. Add ½ cup (120 ml) of the pasta water (scoop some up from the water left in the pasta pot) and mix to thin out the pesto. The sauce should coat the pasta well. If the pasta and sauce look too dry, add more pasta water and mix until the sauce looks creamy and coats the pasta. Add the tomatoes and fresh mozzarella (if using), and toss those into the pasta as well.

6. Serve the spaghetti with extra Parmesan cheese and more fresh basil to sprinkle on top.

CRISPY CHICKEN SAMMIES

Level 3: Challenge Accepted!
Makes 6 sandwiches

Crunchy on the outside and juicy in the center—crispy chicken sandwiches are a fast food favorite for good reason! But, with this recipe, you can learn how to make them at home—which means they are healthier and more delicious! Plus, whipping them up yourself means you get to customize your sandwich however you'd like. My kids love to make their own "special sauce" for these sandwiches by equal parts mayo and ketchup. What will you put on your custom sandwich?

Get Ready!

Grab a liquid measuring cup, a knife and cutting board, an air fryer or baking sheet, 2 plates, a fork, tongs, an instant-read thermometer and measuring spoons.

Get Set!

1½ cups (84 g) panko breadcrumbs

1 tsp kosher salt

½ tsp garlic powder

½ tsp paprika

¼ tsp ground black pepper

2 tbsp (30 ml) extra virgin olive oil

1 large egg

⅓ cup (80 ml) plain yogurt

3 thinly sliced chicken breast cutlets (about 1½ pounds [680 g]), cut in half

6 potato buns or whole wheat hamburger buns

Topping Ideas

Sliced tomato

Lettuce

Pickles

Ketchup and/or mayo

Go!

1. You can use the oven or an air fryer to cook the chicken. If using the oven, preheat it to 425°F (220°C).

2. Place 2 shallow plates or containers on the counter. Add the breadcrumbs, salt, garlic powder, paprika and pepper to one plate. Mix with a fork to combine the ingredients. Drizzle the breadcrumbs with the oil and mix again. You may want to use your hands to really get the oil evenly mixed in.

3. On the other plate, mix the egg and yogurt with the fork until evenly combined. Using tongs, place a piece of chicken in the egg mixture, turning it over and making sure it's completely covered. Then transfer the chicken to the breadcrumbs and flip it around to coat on all sides. You may need to use your hands to help press the crumbs onto the chicken. Transfer the breaded chicken to the baking sheet or directly into your air fryer basket. Repeat with the remaining pieces of chicken, placing them in an even layer. Once you've coated all the chicken, wash your hands.

4. To air fry, cook the chicken at 400°F (200°C) for 15 minutes, flipping the chicken when there is 7 minutes of cook time left. Depending on the size of your air fryer, you may have to cook the chicken in two batches. To bake in the oven, use oven mitts to place the baking sheet in the oven and bake for 20 minutes, or until the chicken is cooked through and golden brown. Insert the tip of an instant read thermometer halfway into the chicken. It is fully cooked when it is at least 165°F (75°C).

5. Assemble the sandwiches by placing a piece of warm crispy chicken on a bun and adding your desired toppings.

Safety First! Raw Chicken ⊙⊙⊙⊙⊙ ⊙⊙⊙⊙⊙

Sometimes uncooked chicken can make people sick. Always wash your hands and anything that comes in contact with raw chicken, and use a thermometer to make sure it's cooked to 165°F (75°C).

MINI DEEP-DISH PIZZAS

Level 3: Challenge Accepted!
Makes 12

Love pizza? You have to make these cute little cups of cheesy goodness! The recipe starts by making homemade pizza dough, but without having to wait a few hours for it to rise! This dough recipe uses baking powder as the leavening agent (what makes the dough rise) instead of yeast. Like pepperoni, veggies or other toppings on your pizza? Add whatever you like on top of the cheese before you add the sauce.

Get Ready!

Grab a liquid measuring cup, a food processor or a large bowl, a large wooden spoon, a small bowl, a pastry brush, a small knife, a muffin tin and dry measuring cups and spoons.

Get Set!

For the Dough

1 cup (125 g) all-purpose flour, plus extra for dusting

1½ cups (180 g) whole wheat flour or all-purpose flour

1 tbsp (14 g) baking powder

½ tsp salt

1 cup (240 ml) warm water

2 tbsp (30 ml) extra virgin olive oil

1 tbsp (15 ml) honey

Go!

1. Preheat the oven to 400°F (200°C).

2. To make the dough in a food processor, add the all-purpose flour, whole wheat flour, baking powder and salt to the bowl fitted with the metal blade. Place the top on the food processor and press the pulse button a few times to mix in the ingredients. In a liquid measuring cup, mix the warm water, olive oil and honey. Pour the liquid into the food processor, close the lid, turn the machine on and let the dough mix for 1 minute, or until a ball of dough forms.

3. To make dough by hand, add the flours, baking powder and salt to a large bowl. Mix with a large wooden spoon. In a liquid measuring cup, mix the warm water, olive oil and honey. Pour the liquid into the bowl and use the spoon to stir everything together into a shaggy dough. This will take a little time and a good amount of stirring, but it will come together eventually (approximately 5 to 10 minutes).

4. Once you have a rough ball of dough, dust your counter with flour and place the dough on the flour. If the dough is very sticky, dust the top of the dough with flour too. Use the flat part of your hands to knead the dough for 1 to 2 minutes, or until it's smooth and not too sticky. Set the dough aside to rest for 5 minutes.

(continued)

For the Pizzas

1 tbsp (15 ml) olive oil

1½ cups (168 g) shredded mozzarella cheese

1 cup (240 ml) marinara or pizza sauce

2 tbsp (13 g) grated Parmesan cheese

5. To assemble the pizzas, add the olive oil to a small bowl. Use a pastry brush to liberally grease the muffin tin with the oil. Brush the inside of each cup as well as the top of the muffin tin. You'll need the remaining oil, so don't discard it.

6. Roll the ball of pizza dough into a 10- to 12-inch (25- to 30-cm) log shape. (This will make it easier to cut into equal-sized pieces.) Divide the dough into 12 pieces, by first cutting the dough log in half. Then, cut each of those pieces in half. At this point you should have 4 equal pieces. Cut each of those pieces into 3 pieces.

7. With your fingers, press one piece of dough out into a 3-inch (8-cm) circle. Press the circle of dough into the bottom and up the sides of one muffin cup. Repeat with the remaining dough.

8. In each cup, place 2 heaping tablespoons (15 g) of shredded mozzarella, desired toppings, and then 1 tablespoon (15 ml) of sauce. Brush the top of the pizza crust with any oil remaining in the little bowl and sprinkle the crust and the top of each pizza with a big pinch of Parmesan.

9. Use oven mitts to carefully transfer the muffin tin to the oven. Bake for 12 minutes, or until the crusts are golden brown. Carefully remove the pan from the oven and allow it to sit for at least 10 minutes before removing from the pan and serving.

MILD-BUT-MIGHTY CHILI

with Easy cheesy Cornbread

Level 3: Challenge Accepted!
Makes 4 servings

"This is the best dinner ever!" My nine- and seven-year-old children exclaimed the first time we made this recipe together. This chili is full of savory flavor and perfect for piling with all your favorite toppings, like cheese, guacamole and sour cream. A box of jazzed-up cornbread is super yummy on its own but tastes even better paired with this homemade chili.

MILD-BUT-MIGHTY CHILI (CONTINUED)
with Easy Cheesy Cornbread

Get Ready!

For the Cornbread: Grab an 8" or 9" (20- or 23-cm) square baking pan, a large bowl, a whisk, a rubber spatula or spoon and measuring cups.

For the Chili: Grab a liquid measuring cup, a knife and cutting board, a colander, a large pot, a wooden spoon and dry measuring cups and spoon.

Get Set!

For the Cornbread

Oil spray or butter, for greasing the pan

1 (15-oz [425-g]) box cornbread mix, plus ingredients listed on the box recipe

1½ cups (170 g) shredded Cheddar cheese

Optional add-ins: 1 cup (136 g) frozen corn kernels and ¼ cup (12 g) snipped chives or sliced scallions

Go!

1. To make the cornbread, preheat the oven according to the package instructions and grease a baking pan with oil spray or butter.

2. Mix up the cornbread batter according to the instructions on the box. Stir in the shredded cheese and any additional add-ins you'd like. Spread the batter in the prepared pan and use oven mitts to transfer the pan to the oven. Bake the cornbread until golden brown and cooked through (see package for time estimate), and then ask a grown-up for help taking the pan out of the oven. Set the pan aside on a cooling rack.

3. While the cornbread bakes, start the chili. Add the oil to a large soup pot, place the pot on the stove and turn the heat to medium. Add the onion and pepper. Cook the veggies, stirring every so often, for 5 minutes, or until they are softened and begin to brown.

4. Add the ground meat and use a wooden spoon to break the meat up into crumbles as it browns. Cook and stir until there's no more pink color left in the meat.

5. Sprinkle in the salt, chili powder, cumin, paprika and garlic powder. Add the tomato paste and stir everything together. Allow the tomato paste and spices to cook into the meat for 1 minute.

1 tbsp (15 ml) extra virgin olive oil

1 cup (160 g) chopped onion

1½ cups (224 g) small-diced bell pepper (from 1 medium pepper)

1 lb (454 g) lean ground beef or ground turkey

2 tsp (12 g) kosher salt

2 tsp (4 g) mild chili powder

1 tsp ground cumin

1 tsp paprika

2 tsp (6 g) garlic powder

1 tbsp (16 g) tomato paste

2 cups (480 ml) water

2 (15-oz [425-g]) cans pinto, black or kidney beans, drained and rinsed

1½ cups (360 ml) jarred mild salsa

Topping Ideas

Shredded Cheddar cheese

Diced tomatoes or salsa

Guacamole or diced avocado

Sour cream or Greek yogurt

Hot sauce

6. Stir in the water, beans and salsa. Lower the heat to low and let the pot slowly simmer for 20 minutes.

7. Turn off the heat and carefully ladle the chili into bowls. Add any toppings that you'd like. Cut the cooled cornbread into squares and serve it with the chili.

Mix It Up! ⊙⊙⊙⊙⊙ ⊙⊙⊙⊙⊙⊙⊙⊙⊙⊙ ⊙⊙⊙⊙⊙

Want a vegetarian chili? Leave out the ground meat and add an extra can of beans to the pot. You could also replace some of the beans with canned chickpeas or lentils!

ULTIMATE BURGERS
with Toppings Bar

Level 3: Challenge Accepted!
Makes 4 burgers

Burger lovers, this one's for you! We are keeping the patties simple because this meal is all about the toppings bar and homemade special sauce. Having more friends and family over? You can easily double this recipe and make it a burger party everyone will flip over!

Get Ready!

Grab a liquid measuring cup, a knife and cutting board, a small bowl, a whisk, a large bowl, 2 plates, a large cast-iron skillet or any large skillet, a spatula, an instant-read thermometer and measuring spoons.

Get Set!

For the Special Sauce

½ cup (120 ml) mayonnaise

¼ cup (60 ml) ketchup

2 tbsp (30 g) sweet pickle relish

For the Burger Patties

1 lb (454 g) ground beef

½ tsp kosher salt

¼ tsp ground black pepper

¼ tsp garlic powder

8 slices American or Cheddar cheese (optional)

For Serving

4 sesame seed burger buns (or any type)

8 slices cooked bacon

2 large tomatoes, sliced

Bibb lettuce

Pickles and/or pickled onions or thinly sliced fresh onion (optional)

Go!

1. To make the special sauce, add the mayonnaise, ketchup and relish to a small bowl. Mix until the ingredients are combined, and then place in the fridge until you are ready to serve the burgers.

2. To make the patties, place the ground beef in a large bowl. Sprinkle the meat with the salt, pepper and garlic powder. Using your clean hands, mix everything together gently, just until the seasoning is mixed through the meat. You don't want to overmix the meat or it will get tough.

3. Pat the meat into an even layer, and then use the side of your hand to mark the meat in half and then again in half in the other direction so that you can see 4 equal portions of meat.

4. Use your hands to scoop out one portion of the meat, gently roll it into a ball, and then pat it out into a flat burger shape. To make sure the burgers don't dome up in the center while cooking, make the center of the burger a little thinner than the sides. Set the burger patty onto a plate, and then form three more burger patties with the remaining meat. Wash your hands really well!

5. Heat a large skillet over medium-high heat. Use a spatula to place the burgers into the hot pan. Cook the burgers for 3 to 5 minutes per side. If using cheese, place 2 slices of cheese on top of each burger right after you flip it to cook on the second side.

6. When done, the temperature of the center of the burger taken with an instant read thermometer should be 150 to 155°F (66 to 68°C) for medium-well (a little bit of pink inside) and 160 to 165°F (71 to 75°C) for well-done (no pink inside).

7. For serving, bring the buns on a clean plate over to the pan with the burgers. Use the spatula to carefully transfer each burger from the pan onto a bun. Place all the toppings onto a serving platter for everyone to top their own burgers as they'd like.

THREE-CHEESE LASAGNA

Level 3: Challenge Accepted!
Makes 6 servings

Can I tell you a secret? Lasagna isn't that hard to make—especially when you use no-boil noodles—but it looks super impressive when you serve it for dinner! Although lasagna is pretty easy to put together, it does take a little while in the oven, so just make sure you plan ahead. I like to add some frozen spinach in with the cheese mixture. You can't taste it that much, and it adds some nice green color and tons of nutrients. Serve the cheesy lasagna with a Caesar salad (a bag mix is totally fine!) and your family will be amazed with your Italian feast!

Get Ready!

Grab a liquid measuring cup, a small bowl (for the eggs), a 9 x 13" (23 x 33-cm) baking dish, pastry brush (optional), a large bowl, a spoon, aluminum foil, knife or spatula and dry measuring cups and spoons.

Get Set!

Oil spray or 1 tbsp (15 ml) olive oil

1 (8–10-oz [226–283-g]) package frozen spinach, defrosted

1 (16-oz [454-g]) container ricotta cheese

2 large eggs, cracked into a small bowl

¼ cup (25 g) grated Parmesan cheese

½ tsp garlic powder

¼ tsp kosher salt

¼ tsp ground black pepper

2½ cups (280 g) shredded mozzarella cheese, divided

3 cups (720 ml) marinara or pasta sauce, divided

1 package no-boil lasagna noodles

Go!

1. Preheat the oven to 375°F (190°C). Grease a 9 x 13-inch (23 x 33-cm) baking dish with oil spray or by brushing with olive oil.

2. Place the defrosted spinach in a clean kitchen towel or a few layers of paper towels and squeeze all the water out of the spinach over the sink.

3. In a large bowl, add the spinach, ricotta cheese, eggs, Parmesan cheese, garlic powder, salt, pepper and 2 cups (226 g) of the shredded mozzarella cheese. Use a spoon to stir until all the ingredients are combined.

4. Spread 1 cup (240 ml) of the marinara sauce on the bottom of your baking dish. Cover the bottom of the pan with lasagna noodles. You may have to break some to make them fit. Spread about one-third of the spinach and cheese mixture over the lasagna sheets. This is layer one.

5. Repeat the process to make the second layer, using ½ cup (120 ml) of marinara sauce, lasagna sheets and one-third of the spinach mixture. Do that one more time to make the third layer.

6. For the top layer, place lasagna sheets to cover the cheese, and then spread over the remaining marinara sauce. Cover the pan tightly with a sheet of aluminum foil. The pan will be heavy, so ask a grown-up for help placing the pan in the oven.

7. Bake for 40 minutes. Once the bake time is up, ask the grown-up to help you remove the pan from the oven—now it will be both heavy and hot! Sprinkle the top of the lasagna with the remaining mozzarella cheese. Have your grown-up helper place the pan back in the oven. Bake for 10 minutes, or until the cheese on top is melted and bubbly.

8. Allow the lasagna to cool for 10 to 15 minutes, and then slice into squares and serve.

OVEN-BAKED CORN DOGS

Level 3: Challenge Accepted!
Makes 8

You don't have to wait for a trip to the fair to enjoy corn dogs! Fluffy cornbread baked around your favorite hot dog—it's a tasty combo perfect for a fun family dinner or friendly get together. Serve with your favorite sauces, like ketchup and mustard, for dipping plus some easy sides like barbecue baked beans and simple coleslaw or salad.

Get Ready!

Grab a small bowl (for the eggs), a liquid measuring cup, a baking sheet, parchment paper, 8 wooden ice pop sticks, a small plate, a large bowl, a rubber spatula or wooden spoon, a spoon and dry measuring cups and spoons.

Get Set!

8 beef, turkey or vegetarian hot dogs

1½ cups + 2 tbsp (204 g) all-purpose flour, divided

⅔ cup (81 g) fine yellow cornmeal

2 tsp (9 g) baking powder

2 tsp (10 g) sugar

½ tsp kosher salt

⅔ cup (160 ml) milk (any type)

2 eggs, cracked into a small bowl

2 tsp (10 ml) vegetable or canola oil

Ketchup and/or mustard, for serving

Go!

1. Preheat the oven to 375°F (190°C). Line the baking sheet with parchment paper.

2. Carefully insert an ice pop stick about halfway through each hot dog. There should be 1½ inches (4 cm) of the stick left to use as a handle. Place the hot dogs on the baking sheet.

3. Place 2 tablespoons (16 g) of the flour on a small plate and set aside. Add the remaining flour to a large bowl. Mix in the cornmeal, baking powder, sugar and salt until all the dry ingredients are well combined.

4. Add the milk, eggs and oil to the bowl and stir to combine. You should have a thick batter.

5. Roll each hot dog in the flour on the plate, tapping off any excess. (This will help the batter stick better.) Holding the stick, dip the hot dog into the cornbread batter and roll it around to coat. This can be a little tricky, so use a spoon or a finger to spread the batter all around the hot dog until the hot dog is completely surrounded. Place the coated hot dog on the baking sheet and repeat the process with the remaining hot dogs. Spread the hot dogs out on the baking sheet so they have plenty of room in between them.

6. Use oven mitts to transfer the baking sheet to the oven. Bake for 20 minutes, or until the cornbread is golden brown and cooked through. Ask a grown-up for help removing the pan from the oven. Cool for 10 to 15 minutes, and serve the corn dogs hot with ketchup and/or mustard for dipping.

SHRIMP CALIFORNIA ROLL SUSHI BOWLS

◇ ◇ ◇

Level 3: Challenge Accepted!
Makes 4 servings

You can have all the yummy flavors of your favorite sushi roll BUT in a totally easy, customizable bowl form! Fluffy sushi rice is the base for flavorful shrimp and any veggies and toppings you'd like. This dinner is easy enough for any weeknight but also special enough to wow friends and family. Put everything out on the counter and let the sushi bowl creation begin!

Get Ready!

Grab a large liquid measuring cup, a fine-mesh strainer, a medium pot with a lid, a wooden spoon, a knife and cutting board, a medium bowl, a spoon and dry measuring cups and spoons.

Get Set!

2 cups (400 g) sushi rice

2¼ cups (540 ml) water

1 lb (454 g) cooked, peeled and deveined shrimp, defrosted if frozen

2 tsp (10 ml) low-sodium soy sauce, plus extra for serving

1 tbsp (15 ml) mayonnaise

1 tbsp (15 ml) sweet chili sauce

½–1 tsp Asian-style hot sauce such as sriracha (optional)

3 tbsp (45 ml) seasoned rice vinegar or 3 tbsp (45 ml) rice vinegar mixed with 2 tsp (10 g) sugar and ½ tsp salt

½ English cucumber, diced

1 ripe avocado, diced

1 cup (93 g) shelled edamame (optional)

1 cup (110 g) shredded carrot

2 tbsp (18 g) sesame seeds or furikake seasoning

Nori (seaweed) sheets or toasted seaweed snacks, cut into thin strips

Go!

1. Place the rice in a fine-mesh strainer and rinse it under cold water for 1 minute. Tap the bottom of the strainer with the palm of your hand until water no longer falls from the strainer (it needs to be well drained). Transfer the rice to a medium pot and pour in the water. Bring the mixture to a full boil over high heat. After it starts boiling, give the rice a stir, loosening any pieces that may be stuck to the bottom. Reduce the heat to low, cover the pot with the lid and simmer for 15 minutes. Remove the pot from the heat (keep the lid on), and let it rest for 15 minutes. (Alternatively, you can cook the rice in a rice cooker according to the machine instructions.)

2. Pat the shrimp dry with paper towels to remove any extra moisture. Chop the shrimp into bite-sized pieces, discarding the tail shells if they are still on. Place the chopped shrimp in a medium bowl. Add the soy sauce, mayo, sweet chili sauce and hot sauce (if using). Toss to coat and place the bowl in the fridge to chill until ready to serve. (You could also mix the sauce ingredients in a small bowl and serve them on the side instead.)

3. Gently stir the seasoned rice vinegar into the cooked sushi rice. Divide the rice into 4 plates or shallow bowls, or transfer the rice to a large bowl for everyone to serve themselves family-style.

4. To serve, place the cucumber, avocado, edamame and carrot in separate bowls with spoons for scooping. Top the rice with the shrimp and desired toppings and sprinkle with sesame seeds/furikake and the strips of seaweed.

SUPERSTAR CHICKEN POT PIE ◇ ◇

Level 3: Challenge Accepted!
Makes 4–6 servings

Comfort food to the max! This stellar pot pie is filled with tender chicken and veggies wrapped in a creamy, dreamy sauce. To make this dish extra special, we cut store-bought pie dough into cute little stars that bake up into the perfect golden-brown pie topping. You can also top the pot pie with the whole, rolled-out layer of dough to get extra crust in each bite. You are going to want to make this super supper all year long!

Get Ready!

Grab a small bowl (for the egg), a large liquid measuring cup, a large soup pot or Dutch oven, tongs, a plate, a wooden spoon, a fork or knife, a 9 x 13" (23 x 33–cm) baking dish/casserole dish, a star (or other shape) cookie cutter, a pastry brush and dry measuring cups and spoons.

Get Set!

1½ lb (680 g) uncooked boneless, skinless chicken thighs

1 cup (240 ml) chicken broth

2 cups (250 g) frozen mixed vegetables such as carrots, corn, green beans and peas

3 tbsp (24 g) cornstarch

2½ cups (600 ml) milk (2% or whole)

1 tsp onion powder

1 tsp garlic powder

¼ tsp poultry seasoning

¼ tsp ground black pepper

½ tsp kosher salt

1 tbsp (14 g) butter

1 (14–16-oz [397–454-g]) package (2 rolls) refrigerated pie crust dough

1 egg, cracked into a small bowl

Go!

1. Preheat the oven to 425°F (220°C).

2. Place a large pot onto the stove and use tongs to transfer the chicken into the pot. Pour the chicken broth over the chicken and turn the heat to medium-high.

3. Cover the pot and let the broth come up to a simmer. Turn the heat down to medium-low, and cook for 8 to 10 minutes or until cooked through. Use clean tongs to transfer the cooked chicken to a plate, leaving the liquid in the pot. Set the chicken aside to cool.

4. Turn the heat to medium-high and stir the frozen vegetables into the liquid.

5. In a large liquid measuring cup, add the cornstarch and milk and whisk until the cornstarch is dissolved. Pour the mixture into the pot. Stir in the onion powder, garlic powder, poultry seasoning, pepper and salt. Allow the liquid to come up to a simmer and begin to thicken. Reduce the heat to medium-low and let the sauce simmer while you shred or chop the cooked chicken into bite-sized pieces.

6. Add the shredded chicken to the pot and stir in the butter.

7. Turn off the heat and ladle the chicken filling into a large casserole dish. You can also ask a grown-up to help you pick up the pot and pour the filling into the dish. Set aside.

8. Unroll the pie dough onto your counter or work surface. Use cookie cutters to cut out stars of different sizes or whatever shapes you'd like. Place the pie dough shapes onto the chicken filling. Beat the egg with a fork and use the pastry brush to brush each pie dough shape with the egg. (This helps them get nice and brown in the oven.)

9. Use oven mitts to transfer the baking dish to the oven or ask a grown-up for help. Bake for 15 minutes, or until the crust is golden brown. Let the pie cool for 15 minutes before scooping it onto plates and serving.

MIC DROP DESSERTS

These sweet treats are going to make you and the lucky people you share them with oh, so happy! There's such a tasty variety of cookies, simple no-bake sweets and decadent cakes in this chapter that you'll find the perfect thing to bake up for any occasion. Best of all, these dessert recipes are (secretly) easy to whip up but will make you look like a top pastry chef. Get ready to take a bow during the standing ovation!

CHOCOLATE PEANUT BUTTER CRISPY TREATS

Level 1: Easy-Peasy
Makes 16 squares

Chocolate and peanut butter are a match made in heaven. If you like peanut butter cups and rice crispy treats, you have to make this recipe ASAP! And these treats couldn't be easier to make. Just stir everything together in one bowl and press it into a pan. You could stop there, but why not add an extra layer of melted chocolate to the top and take these treats to the next level of chocolate awesomeness?

Get Ready!

Grab a liquid measuring cup, a 9 x 13" (23 x 33–cm) baking dish or cake pan, parchment paper or aluminum foil, a large microwave-safe bowl, a large spoon, a medium microwave-safe bowl, a knife and dry measuring cups and spoons.

Get Set!

Oil spray

⅔ cup (160 ml) honey

⅔ cup (172 g) natural, creamy peanut butter

2 tbsp (11 g) unsweetened cocoa powder

1 tsp vanilla extract

¼ tsp salt (skip if peanut butter is salted)

6 cups (150 g) crispy rice cereal

1 cup (168 g) semisweet chocolate chips

1 tsp vegetable or coconut oil

Go!

1. Spray a 9 x 13–inch (23 x 33–cm) baking pan with oil spray and make a "sling" by placing a sheet of parchment paper or aluminum foil on the bottom and up the sides.

2. In a large microwave-safe bowl, add the honey and peanut butter. Place the bowl in the microwave and heat on high for 1 minute. Carefully remove the bowl with a towel (it might be hot). Add the cocoa powder, vanilla and salt and stir until smooth.

3. Add the rice cereal to the bowl and stir until all the cereal is coated in the peanut butter mixture.

4. Dump the coated cereal into your prepared baking dish. Spread it out as evenly as possible. Pack the mixture really well so it sticks together and will form even bars when cut. A great way to do this is to lay another sheet of parchment on top and use the bottom of a measuring cup to pack and flatten the surface of the treats.

5. In a medium microwave-safe bowl, add the chocolate chips and oil. Microwave for 1 minute, and then stir until fully melted. If the chocolate is still too cool, place back in the microwave for 30 seconds.

6. Drizzle the melted chocolate over the top of the mixture in the dish. Chill the dish in the fridge for 20 to 30 minutes, or until the chocolate and cereal mixture are set and hardened. Use the sides of the parchment paper or foil to remove the block of cereal treats from the pan, and then cut the bars into 16 squares. (You may need to have a grown-up help you with this part since a large knife works best.) Serve right away or store in the fridge for up to 1 week.

CHEESECAKE-STUFFED STRAWBERRIES

Level 1: Easy-Peasy
Makes 15–18 berries

Take plain old strawberries from simply sweet to spectacular with this crazy-delicious twist! Fresh strawberries are topped with crushed graham crackers and an easy cheesecake filling made from whipped cream cheese (so there's no mixer needed!). Who knew dessert could be so simple?! Perfect for a party or just a regular Saturday—these strawberries are too good not to share!

Get Ready!

Grab a liquid measuring cup, 2 resealable plastic bags, a knife or paring knife and a cutting board, a large plate, a medium bowl, a spoon, a piping bag (optional), clean kitchen scissors and dry measuring cups and spoons.

Get Set!

1 whole graham cracker

1 lb (454 g) fresh strawberries, rinsed and dried

1 (8-oz [226-g]) container whipped cream cheese

¼ cup (60 ml) maple syrup, honey or ¼ cup (30 g) powdered sugar

½ tsp vanilla extract

Go!

1. Place the graham cracker in a plastic bag and make sure to seal the bag well. Bash the graham cracker up into crumbs with the back of a measuring cup.

2. Cut off the green leaves and stems of the strawberries, and then cut off a little bit of the tip off the strawberries so they can sit flat on a large plate. Use a ½-teaspoon measuring spoon to scoop out a little bit of the larger end of the strawberry where the green part used to be. This is where the filling is going to go. If it's a little too tricky to scoop out, that's okay. You can just place the filling right on top of the strawberry and it will taste just as yummy.

3. Once all of the strawberries are prepped, place them on a plate with the larger part of the strawberry facing up.

4. In a medium bowl, add the cream cheese, maple syrup and vanilla. Stir vigorously with a spoon until the filling is smooth and all the ingredients are combined.

5. Spoon the filling into a small resealable plastic bag or a piping bag. Push all the filling to a corner of the bag, seal the bag or twist the top, and then snip the corner of the bag.

6. Squeeze to pipe the filling into all of the strawberries. Sprinkle each strawberry with a pinch of graham cracker crumbs. Enjoy right away or refrigerate until serving.

Mix It Up! ◇-◇-◇-◇-◇-◇-◇-◇-◇-◇-◇-◇-◇-◇-◇-◇-

Love chocolate? Melt ¼ cup (42 g) of chocolate chips in the microwave in 15-second bursts until completely melted. Let the chocolate cool, and then stir it into the cheesecake filling or drizzle it on top of the strawberries after filling them. Yum!

NO-BAKE COOKIE DOUGH TRUFFLES

Level 1: Easy-Peasy
Makes 20 truffles

Is there anything better than raw chocolate chip cookie dough? Yes . . . cookie dough that's also dipped in melted chocolate! This soft, sweet cookie dough is made without egg, so it's completely safe to eat. Keep the truffles classic with just the yummy chocolate chips, or go crazy and add sprinkles, chopped nuts, white chocolate . . . whatever you like in your cookies!

Get Ready!

Grab a liquid measuring cup, a large bowl, a rubber spatula or large spoon, a baking sheet or plate that fits in your freezer, parchment paper or wax paper, a small microwave-safe bowl, a fork and dry measuring cups and spoons.

Get Set!

1 stick (½ cup [114 g]) unsalted butter, softened

2 tbsp (28 g) light brown sugar

¼ cup (60 ml) maple syrup

⅛ tsp fine salt

½ tsp vanilla extract

¼ tsp almond extract (optional)

2¼ cups (252 g) almond flour or 1½ cups (188 g) heat-treated all-purpose flour (see below)

1½ cups (252 g) mini chocolate chips, divided

1 tsp coconut oil

Go!

1. In a large bowl, add the butter, brown sugar, maple syrup, salt, vanilla and almond extract (if using). Mix until the ingredients are mostly combined. You may have to mash the butter up against the side of the bowl to make sure it is fully softened.

2. Add the flour and continue to stir until a sticky dough forms. Stir in ½ cup (84 g) of the mini chocolate chips.

3. Line a baking sheet or large plate with parchment paper or wax paper. Roll the cookie dough into tablespoon-sized (15-ml) balls and place the balls onto the lined baking sheet or plate. Place the balls into the freezer for 15 minutes.

4. Add the remaining mini chocolate chips to a small microwave-safe bowl. Heat the chocolate chips in the microwave for 30 seconds, and then remove the bowl with an oven mitt (it might be hot) and use a fork to stir up the chocolate chips. Place the bowl back in the microwave and heat for another 30 seconds, and then remove it and stir in the coconut oil. Continue to stir the melted chocolate until it is very smooth.

5. Remove the cookie dough balls from the freezer and either use a fork to dip them in the melted chocolate or drizzle the melted chocolate over the top. Place the cookie dough truffles back in the freezer for 5 minutes, or until the chocolate is set. Store the cookie dough truffles in a container in the refrigerator or freezer until serving.

Chef Tip: Heat-Treated Flour ◇-◇-◇-◇-◇-◇-◇

Eating uncooked (raw) all-purpose flour can sometimes make people sick. But here's how to make it safe to eat. Place the flour in a large, microwave-safe bowl. Heat the flour in the microwave for 1 minute, stopping at 30 seconds to stir. The flour is safe to use when multiple areas of the flour read at least 165°F (75°C) on an instant-read thermometer. You don't need to go through this process if you are using almond flour.

S'MORES BROWNIE BITES

Level 2: Totally Doable
Makes 24 mini brownies

S'mores! Just saying the word transports us to fun summer nights by a campfire. For this sweet treat, we take that classic flavor combo of graham cracker, chocolate and marshmallows and transform it into bite-sized brownies. The brownies are super fudgy thanks to two "secret" ingredients—almond butter and applesauce—but all you taste is chocolate goodness! Not only do the mini s'mores taste amazing, but they are super photo-worthy and sure to be a hit at any party or family gathering!

Get Ready!

Grab a mini muffin tin, mini paper muffin liners, a small resealable plastic bag, a medium microwave-safe bowl, a spoon, a large bowl, a large spoon and measuring cups and spoons.

Get Set!

4 graham crackers or ¾ cup (60 g) graham cracker crumbs

2 tbsp (28 g) unsalted butter, cut into 4 pieces

1 large egg

½ cup (48 g) natural, unsalted almond butter

⅓ cup (80 ml) unsweetened applesauce

⅓ cup (73 g) light brown sugar

1 tsp vanilla extract

½ tsp baking soda

¼ tsp salt

¼ cup (22 g) Dutch-processed cocoa powder (see page 149 for tips on this type of cocoa powder)

¼ cup (31 g) all-purpose flour

¼ cup (42 g) mini chocolate chips

1 cup (50 g) mini marshmallows

Go!

1. Preheat the oven to 350°F (180°C) and line a mini muffin tin with 24 paper liners.

2. Place the graham crackers into a small resealable plastic bag. Close the bag tightly, then use the bottom of a measuring cup to crush the graham crackers into crumbs.

3. Place the butter in a medium microwave-safe bowl and heat it in the microwave for 30 to 45 seconds, or until melted. Add the graham cracker crumbs to the butter and carefully stir to combine them. It should look like wet sand. Scoop 1 teaspoon of the buttered graham cracker crumbs into the bottom of each muffin cup. You should still have some of the crumb mixture left to use for the top of the brownies. Use the back of the spoon to press the crumbs into the bottom of the cups to pack them down.

4. In a large bowl, stir together the egg, almond butter, applesauce, brown sugar and vanilla. Add the baking soda, salt, cocoa powder, flour and chocolate chips and stir to combine all the ingredients.

5. Using a tablespoon measuring spoon, scoop the brownie batter on top of each of the graham cracker crusts in the muffin tin.

6. Press 2 or 3 mini marshmallows into the top of each brownie, and then sprinkle with a pinch of the remaining graham cracker crumbs.

7. Using oven mitts, carefully place the muffin tin onto the center rack of the oven. Set a timer for 10 minutes, and bake until the marshmallows are golden brown. If the marshmallows aren't browned and the brownie batter still looks wet, set the timer for 2 more minutes and continue to bake.

8. Use oven mitts to remove the pan from the oven, or have a grown-up help you. Allow the brownies to cool in the pan for 15 minutes before removing them and serving.

PUCKER-UP LEMON BARS

Level 2: Totally Doable
Makes 16 small squares

Are you on Team Sweet or Team Sour? When you make this lemony dessert you can be both! These are the perfect easy treats to bring to a friend's house. Just make sure to plan ahead because they need to chill in the fridge for a bit before serving. These are a classic favorite for good reason, so don't be surprised when people start puckering up to give the chef a kiss on the cheek! Mmwah!

Get Ready!

Grab a small bowl (for the eggs), a liquid measuring cup, a zester (optional), a 9" (23-cm) square baking pan, parchment paper, a large microwave-safe bowl, a whisk, a large spoon or rubber spatula, a fork, a citrus squeezer/juicer, a fork, a large bowl, a cutting board and butter knife and dry measuring cups and spoons.

Get Set!

For the Crust

1 stick (½ cup [114 g]) unsalted butter, cut into 8 pieces

¼ cup (50 g) granulated sugar

1 tsp lemon zest (optional)

1 tsp vanilla extract

½ tsp salt

1 cup (125 g) all-purpose flour

For the Filling

1 cup (200 g) granulated sugar

3 tbsp (24 g) all-purpose flour

3 large eggs, cracked into a small bowl

½ cup (120 ml) fresh lemon juice (from 2–3 lemons)

Powdered sugar, for topping

Go!

1. Preheat the oven to 325°F (165°C). Line a 9-inch (23-cm) square baking pan with parchment paper so the paper is hanging over the sides of the pan for easy removal.

2. To make the crust, add the butter to a large, microwave-safe bowl. Place in the microwave for 30 to 45 seconds or until melted. Use an oven mitt to remove the bowl.

3. Add the sugar, lemon zest (if using), vanilla and salt to the bowl with the melted butter. Whisk until the butter and sugar are well combined.

4. Add the flour and mix with a large spoon or rubber spatula until you have a thick dough. Crumble the dough over your prepared pan, and then pat it down to an even layer.

5. Use oven mitts to place the crust in the oven. Set a timer for 12 minutes and bake until the crust is lightly golden brown around the edges. If it's still very pale, set a timer and bake for 2 more minutes. Carefully remove from the oven with oven mitts or ask a grown-up for help. Poke holes all over the top of the crust with a fork, making sure not to go all the way through to the bottom.

6. To make the filling, whisk the sugar and flour together in a large bowl, making sure there aren't any lumps of flour. Whisk in the eggs and lemon juice until everything is well combined. Pour over the warm crust, and use oven mitts to carefully transfer the pan back to the oven.

7. Bake for 16 to 18 minutes, or until the filling is just set. If you tap the pan with an oven mitt, it should jiggle slightly in the center. Carefully remove the pan or ask an adult for help. Allow the bars to cool for at least 2 hours at room temperature, and then put the pan in the fridge to chill for 1 hour.

8. Lift the parchment paper out of the pan, and then transfer to a cutting board. If the bar is stuck, run a butter knife between the bar and the pan to loosen it. Dust with powdered sugar, then cut into squares. The lemon bars are best served chilled.

BIG AND CHEWY CHOCOLATE CHIP COOKIES

Level 2: Totally Doable
Makes 8 large cookies

Ooey, gooey, chewy and GIGANTIC—these chocolate chip cookies are going to be the best cookies you've ever had! Chocolate chip cookies are a crowd favorite for good reason and will instantly put a smile on anyone's face. This cookie recipe couldn't be easier to whip up, and there's no mixer needed. Once you try the original flavor, feel free to give this recipe your own spin. You can find some suggestions for fun mix-ins on page 142.

Get Ready!

Grab a small bowl (for the egg), a baking sheet, parchment paper, a large microwave-safe bowl, a whisk, a large spoon or rubber spatula and measuring spoons and cups.

Get Set!

1 stick (½ cup [114 g]) cold unsalted butter, cut into 8 pieces

¼ cup (50 g) granulated sugar

½ cup (110 g) light brown sugar

1 large egg, cracked into a small bowl

2 tsp (10 ml) vanilla extract

1¾ cups (219 g) all-purpose flour (spooned into the measuring cup and leveled)

½ tsp baking soda

½ tsp kosher salt

1 cup (168 g) semisweet chocolate chips, plus more for topping

Go!

1. Preheat the oven to 350°F (180°C). Line a baking sheet with parchment paper for easy cleanup.

2. Add the butter to a large microwave-safe bowl. Heat the butter in the microwave until it is softened, about 40 seconds. It's okay if the butter is slightly melted.

3. Add the white and brown sugars to the butter, and whisk them all together for 30 seconds, or until they are well combined and look creamy.

4. Add the egg and vanilla and whisk until well combined. Tap your whisk on the side of the bowl to remove any batter.

5. Add the flour, baking soda and salt. Switch to a large spoon or rubber spatula and stir everything together. Once the flour is almost fully mixed in, stir in the chocolate chips.

6. Use a ¼-cup (60-ml) measuring cup to scoop heaping ¼-cup (60-g) portions of the cookie dough onto the baking sheet. Press the top of each dough ball down slightly, and then place 4 to 5 more chocolate chips on the top.

(continued)

BIG AND CHEWY CHOCOLATE CHIP COOKIES (CONTINUED)

7. Use oven mitts to place the baking sheet onto the center rack of the oven. Set a timer for 11 minutes and bake until lightly golden brown around the edges. If the cookies still look pale around the edges, set a timer for 1 minute and continue to bake. The center of the cookies will still look a little underdone, and that's okay.

8. Allow the cookies to cool on the baking sheet, and then enjoy! Store the cookies in an airtight container for 2 days.

Mix It Up! ◇·◇

Replace the chocolate chips with one of the flavor combos below:

» The Kitchen Sink: ¼ cup (25 g) crushed potato chips, ½ cup (120 g) toffee pieces, ½ cup (84 g) chocolate chips

» Candy Cane Chocolate Chip: ¼ cup (42 g) crushed candy canes, ½ cup (84 g) white chocolate chips, ½ cup (84 g) chocolate chips

» Monster Cookies: ½ cup (102 g) M&M's® candies, ¼ cup (15 g) crushed pretzels and ½ cup (84 g) peanut butter chips

CHURRO PASTRY TWISTS

with chocolate Dipping sauce

Level 2: Totally Doable
Makes 16 twists and 1½ cups (360 ml) sauce

Crispy, sweet, flaky pastry dunked in warm chocolate sauce—these churros are yummy in so many ways! Traditionally, churros are a fried dough served in Spain, Portugal and Latin American countries. But for this recipe, we are using store-bought puff pastry as a smart shortcut to get all that amazing churro flavor without the hassle of frying.

Get Ready!

For the Churros: Grab a baking sheet, parchment paper, 2 small microwave-safe bowls, a large cutting board, a pastry brush, a rolling pin (optional), a pizza wheel or paring knife and measuring cups and spoons.

For the Chocolate Dip: Grab a liquid measuring cup, a small pot, a small bowl, a whisk, a rubber spatula and dry measuring cups and spoons.

Get Set!

For the Churros

1 stick (½ cup [114 g]) unsalted butter

¼ cup (50 g) granulated sugar

1 tsp ground cinnamon or pumpkin pie spice

Pinch of salt

1 (17-oz [490 g]) package frozen puff pastry, defrosted according to package directions but still cold

Go!

1. Preheat the oven to 400°F (200°C). Line a baking sheet with parchment paper.

2. To make the churros, add the butter to a small, microwave-safe bowl. Heat until melted, about 30 to 40 seconds. In a second small bowl, mix the sugar, cinnamon and salt.

3. If the puff pastry gets too warm, it will be hard to work with, so place it in the refrigerator for 20 minutes. Lay 1 sheet of the pastry flat on a cutting board, unfolding or unrolling as needed.

4. Brush the melted butter all over the top of the pastry sheet, covering it completely. Sprinkle half of the sugar mixture all over the butter.

5. Place the second sheet of puff pastry on top of the first. Sprinkle the top with the remaining sugar mixture. Press down gently or use a rolling pin to help the sugar stick to the pastry. Fold the dough in half widthwise, like you are closing a book, and press down again.

6. Using a pizza wheel or knife, cut the dough into 16 equal pieces. (Cut into equal quarters, and then cut each quarter into 4 pieces.)

7. Twist the strips together 5 to 6 times until the two layers of dough are completely twisted. Pinch both ends of the strips, and then place them on the baking sheet. Place the twists close together but not touching.

For the Chocolate Dipping Sauce

1 cup (240 ml) milk (any type), divided

1 cup (168 g) chocolate chips

1 tbsp (8 g) cornstarch

8. Use oven mitts to transfer the baking sheet to the oven. Bake for 13 to 15 minutes, or until the twists are very golden brown. Carefully remove the pan with oven mitts or ask a grown-up for help.

9. While the twists bake, make the chocolate sauce. Add ½ cup (120 ml) of the milk and the chocolate to a small pot. In a small bowl, dissolve the cornstarch in the remaining milk by whisking them together. Set the pot on the stovetop over medium heat. Hold the pot handle with an oven mitt and use a rubber spatula to stir constantly once the chocolate starts to melt. Once the chocolate is melted, stir in the cornstarch-milk mixture and continue to stir for 5 minutes, or until the chocolate sauce starts to bubble gently and thicken. Remove the pot from the heat and set aside until ready to serve.

10. Place the warm twists onto a plate and spoon the warm chocolate sauce into a bowl for dipping.

DISAPPEARING BLUEBERRY COBBLER

Level 2: Totally Doable
Makes 6 servings

This fun and fruity dessert is like a magic trick! I call it "disappearing" blueberry cobbler for two reasons: One, you sprinkle the blueberries on top of the easy cobbler batter, and when it bakes, the blueberries disappear under the sweet, buttery cake. Two, this dessert is so flavorful and delicious it's gobbled up and disappears in no time! Top the warm cobbler with vanilla ice cream and wait for your family to ask you to make this recipe over and over again.

Get Ready!

Grab a liquid measuring cup, deep-dish pie plate or a 1-quart (960-ml) baking dish, a small microwave-safe bowl, a large bowl, a whisk, a rubber spatula, a butter knife and dry measuring cups and spoons.

Get Set!

Oil spray

3 tbsp (42 g) butter

1 cup (125 g) all-purpose flour

½ cup (100 g) granulated sugar

2 tsp (9 g) baking powder

¼ tsp salt

1 cup (240 ml) milk (any type)

1 tsp vanilla extract

2 cups (296 g) fresh or frozen blueberries

Vanilla ice cream, for serving (optional)

Go!

1. Preheat the oven to 350°F (180°C). Grease a deep-dish pie plate or a square baking dish with oil spray.

2. Place the butter in a small microwave-safe bowl and heat in the microwave for 35 to 40 seconds, or until melted. The bowl might be hot, so use an oven mitt to remove it from the microwave.

3. In a large bowl, whisk together the flour, sugar, baking powder and salt.

4. Add the milk, vanilla and melted butter and whisk to combine. It's okay if the batter still has a few small lumps.

5. Pour the batter into your prepared baking dish, using a rubber spatula to get all the batter out of the bowl. Spread the batter into an even layer.

6. Sprinkle the blueberries evenly over the top of the batter.

7. Use oven mitts to transfer the cobbler to the oven. Set a timer for 40 minutes and bake until the top is golden brown and a butter knife inserted into the center comes out without any wet batter on it. If the cobbler still looks underdone, set a timer and bake for 5 more minutes. Ask a grown-up for help with removing the cobbler from the oven.

8. Serve the cobbler warm with a scoop of vanilla ice cream on top, if you'd like.

SECRET INGREDIENT CHOCOLATE "DIRT" CUPS

Level 2: Totally Doable
Makes 4 servings

How fun are these edible dirt cups? You can play a silly prank on your family with this sneaky dessert that is made from chocolate pudding, crushed cookies and gummy worms. Yum! This chocolate pudding is creamy, sweet and decadent, but it's also made from tofu! Wait, tofu?! Yes! Hear me out. Using silken tofu not only makes this dessert more nutritious (tofu is full of protein!), but it also creates the thickest and creamiest texture without all the extra steps of cooking traditional pudding on the stovetop. I promise that all you will taste is sweet chocolate goodness (and not the tofu at all).

Get Ready!

Grab a liquid measuring cup, a small microwave-safe bowl, a food processor or blender, a rubber spatula, 4 glass jars or bowls, a large resealable plastic bag, a spoon and dry measuring cups and spoons.

Get Set!

½ cup (84 g) chocolate chips

1 (14–16-oz [396–454-g]) package silken tofu

⅓ cup (28 g) unsweetened cocoa powder

⅓ cup (80 ml) maple syrup or agave nectar

½ tsp vanilla extract

¼ tsp fine salt

8–10 chocolate cookies, such as Oreo® Chocolate Sandwich Cookies

Gummy worms and/or fresh mint sprigs, for garnishing

Go!

1. Add the chocolate chips to a small microwave-safe bowl. Place the bowl in the microwave and heat in 30-second intervals until the chocolate is melted. Use an oven mitt to remove the bowl because it might be hot.

2. Drain any liquid that's in the package of tofu. With a grown-up's help, make sure a food processor or blender is properly plugged in and fitted with the metal blade. Add the tofu, cocoa powder, maple syrup, vanilla, salt and melted chocolate. Lock the lid and process until all the ingredients are smooth and well combined. You may need to use a rubber spatula to scrape down the sides and process again if anything is stuck.

3. Have a grown-up help you carefully remove the blade from the food processor or blender. Spoon the chocolate pudding into 4 small glass jars or bowls. Cover the containers with plastic wrap and place in the fridge to chill for at least 30 minutes and up to 24 hours.

4. Place the cookies inside a resealable plastic bag and make sure to close it tightly. Use the back of a measuring cup to bash the cookies into crumbles.

5. Once ready to serve, top the chocolate pudding with the cookie crumbles and decorate with 2 to 3 gummy worms and/or sprigs of fresh mint so the cups look like little plants.

Chef Tip: Cocoa Powder ◇-◇-◇-◇-◇-◇-◇-◇-◇-◇

There are two common types of cocoa powder used in baking recipes: natural cocoa powder and Dutch-processed cocoa powder. Both of these are unsweetened. Dutch cocoa is natural cocoa that has been processed to have more of a dark chocolate color and flavor. Since the two kinds of cocoa powder react differently to baking soda and baking powder, it's best to use the kind of cocoa in the ingredient list. However, if you don't have Dutch cocoa, you can use the natural kind. The end result will just have a less fudgy flavor.

FUNFETTI® CUPCAKES

with Easy Vanilla Frosting

Level 3: Challenge Accepted!
Makes 12 cupcakes

What's more fun than cupcakes packed with rainbow sprinkles?? Nothing! You will look and feel like a serious baking rock star when you share these treats with friends and family. Whip up the vanilla frosting and simply spread it on with a butter knife, or if you are feeling fancy, double the frosting recipe and use a piping bag to make a pretty swirl. Either way, be sure to shower them with some extra rainbow sprinkles!

Get Ready!

For the Cupcakes: Grab a liquid measuring cup, a small bowl, a muffin tin, paper liners, a large bowl, a whisk and dry measuring cups and spoons.

For the Frosting: Grab an electric mixer and bowl, a rubber spatula, a piping bag (optional) and measuring cups and spoons.

Get Set!

For the Cupcakes

¾ cup (150 g) granulated sugar

1¼ cups (156 g) all-purpose flour

1 tsp baking powder

¼ tsp baking soda

¼ tsp salt

¾ cup (180 ml) milk (any type)

2 tsp (10 ml) vanilla extract

¼ cup (60 ml) vegetable oil

1 egg, cracked into a small bowl and lightly beaten

½ cup (88 g) rainbow sprinkles, plus extra for decorating

For the Vanilla Frosting

1 stick (½ cup [114 g]) unsalted butter, softened

1 tsp vanilla extract

Pinch of salt

1½ cups (180 g) powdered sugar

1 tbsp (15 ml) milk or cream

Go!

1. Preheat the oven to 350°F (180°C). Place the cupcake liners inside your muffin tin.

2. To make the cupcakes, add the sugar, flour, baking powder, baking soda and salt to a large bowl. Whisk to combine all the ingredients.

3. Add the milk, vanilla, oil and egg. Whisk until everything is combined. Stir in the sprinkles.

4. Use a ¼-cup (60-ml) measuring cup to scoop the batter into the cupcake liners, filling the cups about two-thirds of the way.

5. Use oven mitts to transfer the muffin tin to the center rack of your oven. Bake for 18 minutes, or until the cupcakes are just barely golden brown around the edges and a toothpick inserted into the center of the largest cupcake comes out clean.

6. Remove the pan from the oven with oven mitts or ask an adult for help. Once the cupcakes are cool enough to touch, remove them from the pan. Allow the cupcakes to cool completely before frosting.

7. To make the frosting, add the soft butter to a large bowl or the bowl of your stand mixer. Add the vanilla and salt. Beat the butter with a hand mixer or stand mixer on medium speed. Add the powdered sugar, ½ cup (60 g) at a time, stopping to scrape down the sides and bottom of the bowl to incorporate anything that might be stuck. Add the milk, and then whip the frosting for 30 to 60 seconds, or until it's thick and smooth.

8. Once the cupcakes have cooled completely, spread or pipe the frosting on top of each cupcake and add an extra pinch of rainbow sprinkles to the top. Eat them right away, or if you're making them for a party, store them in the refrigerator, covered, for up to 1 day before serving.

SWEET FRUIT PIZZA

with Sugar Cookie Crust

OMG! This colorful, fruity dessert is a showstopper! You will impress everyone with this cookie pizza and have the best time making it. Flex that creativity and top the giant cookie with a rainbow of fruit, do a holiday color scheme or use whatever combo you enjoy.

Level 3: Challenge Accepted!
Makes 6–8 servings

Get Ready!

Grab a knife and cutting board, parchment paper, clean kitchen scissors, an 8" or 9" (20- or 25-cm) round cake pan, an electric hand mixer and a large bowl or a stand mixer with the paddle attachment, a rubber spatula, a large bowl, a spoon or butter knife and measuring cups and spoons.

Get Set!

For the Cookie Dough Crust

Oil spray

1 stick (½ cup [114 g]) unsalted butter, softened

⅓ cup (66 g) granulated sugar

1 egg

1 tsp vanilla extract

1½ cups (188 g) all-purpose flour

⅛ tsp salt

½ tsp baking powder

For the Frosting

4 oz (113 g) cream cheese, softened

¼ cup (30 g) powdered sugar

¼ tsp vanilla extract

Topping Ideas

Strawberries, orange, pineapple, kiwi, blueberries, blackberries, other fruit of your choice

Go!

1. Preheat the oven to 350°F (180°C). Cut four strips of parchment paper that will fit on the bottom and up the sides of a round cake pan. Spray the cake pan with oil, and then place the parchment strips in the pan. These will act like a sling, so you can easily remove the cookie crust from the pan after it's cooked.

2. To make the cookie dough, you can use an electric mixer or stand mixer, or if you'd prefer, you can use your muscles and make the dough by hand in a large bowl. Add the butter and sugar to a large bowl or the bowl of a stand mixer. Beat for 1 minute, or until it becomes a little lighter in color and fluffy. Add the egg and vanilla and beat again until combined. The egg might make the mixture look curdled and strange, but that's okay. Scrape down the sides of the bowl to make sure no butter is stuck and beat again for 30 seconds.

3. Add the flour, salt and baking powder and slowly mix until all the flour is combined.

4. Dump the dough into your prepared cake pan and use your fingers to press the dough into an even layer. Take your time so the crust will be flat and even.

5. Use oven mitts to transfer the cake pan to the oven. Bake for 15 to 18 minutes, or until the dough is golden brown. Place the pan on a cooling rack and allow the cookie crust to cool completely.

6. While the cookie crust is cooling, make the frosting. In a separate large bowl or the bowl of a stand mixer, place the cream cheese, powdered sugar and vanilla. Using either an electric mixer, a whisk or a stand mixer, beat everything together until smooth. Chill the frosting in the fridge until you are ready to assemble the fruit pizza.

7. Once the crust is cool, spread the frosting evenly over the top and decorate with the sliced fruit however you'd like. Slice the pizza into 6 or 8 wedges and serve.

MINI APPLE HAND PIES

Level 3: Challenge Accepted!
Makes 8

Aren't these tiny pies almost too cute to eat? Forget the fork—you can pick these pies up and eat them with your hands! Store-bought pie dough is a helpful shortcut that will let you concentrate on making your little pies extra pretty. For an even more special treat, serve each pie with a scoop of vanilla ice cream and a drizzle of caramel sauce. Your family and friends will be totally amazed that you made these fancy-looking, finger-licking-good pies!

Get Ready!

Grab a small bowl (for the egg), a baking sheet, parchment paper, a vegetable peeler, a knife and cutting board, a medium bowl, a spoon, a 3" (8-cm) round cookie cutter (or simple round object), a paring knife (optional), a pizza wheel, a fork, a small bowl, a pastry brush and measuring cups and spoons.

Get Set!

For the Pies

1 (14–16-oz [397–454-g]) package (2 rolls) refrigerated pie dough

1 large Granny Smith apple

2 tbsp (28 g) brown sugar

1 tsp lemon juice

¼ tsp cinnamon

Go!

1. Preheat the oven to 350°F (180°C). Line a baking sheet with parchment paper.

2. Leave the rolls of pie dough out on the counter until they are still cold but easy to unroll.

3. Peel the apple, and then chop it into a very small dice, the smallest you can make. Cutting an apple off the core can be tricky, so ask a grown-up for help.

4. Place the chopped apple into a medium bowl with the brown sugar, lemon juice and cinnamon. Stir to coat the apple pieces in all the ingredients.

5. Unroll 1 pie crust and cut it into 8 (3-inch [8-cm]) circles. If you don't have a cookie/biscuit cutter handy, you can use the rim of a glass or small round bowl to mark the circle, and then cut it out with a paring knife. Place the dough circles on a baking sheet.

6. Top each dough circle with a heaping spoonful of the apple mixture.

7. To make a lattice-topped pie, unroll the second pie dough and cut it into ¼-inch (6-mm) strips with a pizza wheel or paring knife. Lay 4 strips of dough over the apples in one direction and then 4 in the opposite direction, making a crosshatch pattern. As you place the strips of dough, pinch off any excess that overhangs the circle, and then press the ends of the strips to the circle of dough so they stay in place. Repeat this with the remaining pies.

(continued)

MINI APPLE HAND PIES (CONTINUED)

For the Topping

1 tbsp (15 g) granulated sugar

⅛ tsp ground cinnamon

1 egg, cracked into a small bowl

8. To make a full crust pie, cut the second pie dough into the same size circles you used for the bottom crust. Use your fingers to pinch the dough out into a slightly bigger circle so it will fit over the apples. Place the dough on top of the apples, and then press the edges down to seal the two pieces together. Use the tines of a fork to seal around the circle, and then make a small cut in the top of the pie to vent air.

9. To make the topping, in a small bowl, mix together the granulated sugar and cinnamon. Beat the egg in its bowl with a fork until it's well blended. Using a pastry brush, generously brush the beaten egg over the dough on top of the pies. Sprinkle a few big pinches of the cinnamon-sugar topping over each pie.

10. Use oven mitts to transfer the baking sheet to the oven. Bake for 20 to 25 minutes, or until the pies are very golden brown. Use oven mitts to carefully remove the pan from the oven or ask a grown-up for help. Let the pies cool for 10 minutes, and then enjoy warm or at room temperature.

Waste Not! ◇◦◇◦◇◦◇◦◇◦◇◦◇◦◇◦◇◦◇◦◇◦◇◦◇◦◇

Make the leftover pie dough scraps into pie dough "cookies" by brushing the dough with the leftover egg wash, sprinkling with the cinnamon-sugar, and then baking at 350°F (180°C) until golden brown.

MINT CHOCOLATE CHIP ICE CREAM CAKE

Level 3: Challenge Accepted!
Makes 1 cake, 6–8 servings

Cookie crumbs, sweet and smooth ice cream plus chocolate chips—this dessert is a dream come true! And what's even more exciting is this recipe will show you how to make your very own ice cream! Without any special equipment needed, too. Don't want mint ice cream? Just leave out the mint extract and green coloring, and you've got seriously delish chocolate chip ice cream.

MINT CHOCOLATE CHIP ICE CREAM CAKE (CONTINUED)

Get Ready!

Grab a liquid measuring cup, a 9" or 10" (23- or 25-cm) round cake pan, plastic wrap, a large resealable bag, a large bowl and an electric hand mixer or a stand mixer with the whisk attachment, a rubber spatula, a cake knife and dry measuring cups and spoons.

Get Set!

16 chocolate sandwich cookies (such as Oreos®) or any chocolate cookies

2 tbsp (30 ml) melted butter

2 cups (480 ml) heavy cream

1 tsp peppermint extract

½ tsp vanilla extract

A few drops of green food coloring

1 (14-oz [396-g]) can sweetened condensed milk

1 cup (168 g) mini or regular chocolate chips

Go!

1. Line a cake pan with plastic wrap so there is plenty of excess hanging over the sides.

2. Place the cookies in a resealable plastic bag, close the bag tightly, and then use the back of a measuring cup to bash the cookies into little crumbs.

3. Open the bag and add the melted butter. Close it back up and shake the cookie crumbs to mix in the butter. Dump the cookie crumbs into the bottom of the lined cake pan, and then press firmly into an even crust layer.

4. To make the ice cream, pour the cream into a large bowl (and use an electric hand mixer) or the bowl of a stand mixer. Beat the cream on medium speed until it begins to thicken. Stop the mixer and add the peppermint extract, vanilla and a drop of green food coloring. You can always add more coloring, so start with just a tiny bit.

5. Continue to beat the cream on medium-high speed until it forms soft peaks. (When you lift up the beaters, a peak should form but fall over at the tip.) This should take about 6 to 7 minutes. Be careful not to overbeat the cream or it will start to curdle.

6. Pour the sweetened condensed milk into the whipped cream, using a rubber spatula to get everything out of the can. Gently fold the sweetened condensed milk into the whipped cream with the spatula until combined. Fold in the chocolate chips.

Topping Ideas

1 cup (168 g) chocolate chips

2 tsp (10 ml) coconut oil

7. Pour the ice cream base into the pan. Fold the overhanging plastic wrap over the top, and then stick the pan in the freezer. Freeze for at least 8 hours, or until solid.

8. If you want to make your cake extra fancy, melt the 1 cup (168 g) of chocolate chips, and then stir in the coconut oil. Drizzle the melted chocolate over the cake, and then place it back in the freezer until ready to serve.

9. Remove the pan from the freezer and unwrap the plastic wrap from the top. Use the ends of the plastic wrap to pull the cake out of the pan. Continue to remove the plastic, and then slide a plate under the cake. Slice the cake into pieces and serve.

Chef Tip: Chill Out! ◇·◇·◇·◇·◇·◇·◇·◇·◇·◇·◇

If it's hot in your kitchen, stick the bowl and beaters of your mixer in the freezer or fridge to chill them before whipping the cream. This will ensure you get light and fluffy whipped cream in no time!

ALLERGY FRIENDLY INDEX

RECIPE NAME	PAGE NUMBER	GLUTEN-FREE	DAIRY-FREE	EGG-FREE	NUT-FREE
Five-Minute Superstar Snacks					
Monster Cookie Energy Balls	Page 26	Use gluten-free oats	Use dairy-free mini chocolate chips	Yes	Use sunflower seed butter or other nut-free butter; use ground flaxseed instead of almond meal
Chocolate Power-Me-Up Smoothie	Page 28	Yes	Use dairy-free milk	Yes	Use sunflower seed butter or tahini
Rainbow Fruit Skewers with Creamy Peanut Butter Dip	Page 30	Yes	Use dairy-free yogurt	Yes	Use sunflower seed butter or other nut-free butter
Vanilla-Berry Shake	Page 32	Yes	Use dairy-free milk, dairy-free Greek-style yogurt and dairy-free whipped topping	Yes	Yes
Rock Star Ranch Dip	Page 34	Yes	Use dairy-free Greek-style yogurt	Use egg-free or vegan mayonnaise	Yes
Trail Mix Popcorn Clusters	Page 36	Use gluten-free pretzels and gluten-free cereal	Use dairy-free chocolate chips	Yes	Use seeds, such as sunflower seeds and pumpkin seeds
Supreme Banana "Dogs"	Page 38	Use gluten-free hot dog buns	Yes (use dairy-free chocolate chips if using for toppings)	Yes	Use sunflower seed butter or other nut-free butter; omit nuts from topping choices
Double Chocolate Mug Cake	Page 40	Use a gluten-free flour blend	Use dairy-free milk and dairy-free chocolate chips	Yes	Yes
Sparkling Raspberry Watermelon Lemonade	Page 42	Yes	Yes	Yes	Yes
Pizza Grilled Cheese, Please!	Page 44	Use gluten-free sandwich bread	Use dairy-free cheese	Yes	Yes
Smashed Guacamole with Easy Baked Chips	Page 46	Use corn (or other gluten-free) tortillas	Yes	Yes	Yes
Caramel Apple "Nachos"	Page 48	Yes	Use dairy-free mini chocolate chips (if using for toppings)	Yes	Use sunflower seed butter or other nut-free butter
Crispy Bean and Cheese Taquitos	Page 50	Use corn (or other gluten-free) tortillas	Use dairy-free (or vegan) cream cheese and dairy-free shredded cheese	Yes	Yes

RECIPE NAME	PAGE NUMBER	GLUTEN–FREE	DAIRY–FREE	EGG–FREE	NUT–FREE
Breakfasts of Champions					
Superhero Smoothie Bowls	Page 54	Yes	Use dairy-free vanilla or Greek-style yogurt and coconut water or dairy-free milk	Yes	Yes
Berry Breakfast Ice Pops	Page 56	Yes	Use dairy-free vanilla yogurt	Yes	Use nut-free granola
Giant Baked Pancake	Page 58	Use a gluten-free flour blend	Use dairy-free milk and dairy-free mini chocolate chips (if using)	Use egg-free or vegan pancake mix	Yes
Fiesta Breakfast Quesadillas	Page 60	Use gluten-free tortillas	Use dairy-free shredded cheese	Use liquid egg replacer (such as Just Egg™ brand)	Yes
PB&J Breakfast Cookies	Page 62	Use a gluten-free flour blend and gluten-free oats	Yes	Use a flax egg: 1 tbsp (10 g) ground flaxseed mixed with 3 tbsp (45 ml) water	Use sunflower seed butter or other nut-free butter
Banana Split Overnight Oats	Page 64	Use gluten-free oats	Use dairy-free milk and dairy-free mini chocolate chips	Yes	Use sunflower seed butter or other nut-free butter; use milk or nut-free milk alternative; omit nuts from toppings
Omelet Bagel Boats	Page 66	Use gluten-free bagels	Use dairy-free shredded cheese	Use liquid egg replacer (such as Just Egg brand)	Yes
Fluffy Chocolate Chip Waffles	Page 68	Use a gluten-free flour blend	Use dairy-free butter, dairy-free milk and dairy-free mini chocolate chips	Substitution not recommended	Yes
Pumpkin French Toast Cupcakes	Page 70	Use gluten-free bread	Use dairy-free milk and dairy-free cream cheese	Substitution not recommended	Yes
Banana Bread Power Bars	Page 72	Use gluten-free oats	Use dairy-free mini chocolate chips	Yes	Yes
Sunnyside Up Breakfast Pizzas	Page 74	Use a gluten-free pizza crust or tortilla	Use dairy-free shredded cheese	Omit eggs	Yes
Apple Cinnamon Streusel Muffins	Page 76	Use a gluten-free flour blend	Use dairy-free butter and dairy-free Greek-style yogurt	Substitution not recommended	Yes
Headliner Lunch Boxes					
Build-Your-Own Mini Tacos	Page 80	Use corn (or other gluten-free) tortillas	Use dairy-free shredded cheese and dairy-free sour cream (if using)	Yes	Yes
Stellar Sandwich Pockets	Page 82	Use gluten-free sandwich bread	Yes	Omit hard-boiled egg	Use sunflower seed butter or other nut-free butter
Waffle-Wich On A Stick	Page 84	Use gluten-free waffles	Use dairy-free cream cheese (or nut/seed butter)	Use egg-free or vegan waffles	Use cream cheese, sunflower seed butter or other nut-free butter
Pizza Lunch Box Muffins	Page 86	Use gluten-free flour blend	Use dairy-free milk	Substitution not recommended	Yes

RECIPE NAME	PAGE NUMBER	GLUTEN–FREE	DAIRY–FREE	EGG–FREE	NUT–FREE
Chicken Caesar Salad Kebabs	Page 88	Use gluten-free bread	Use dairy-free Greek-style yogurt (or mayonnaise) and dairy-free Parmesan-style cheese	Use egg-free or vegan mayonnaise (or Greek yogurt)	Yes
DIY Yogurt Parfaits with Crunchy Maple Granola	Page 90	Use gluten-free oats	Use dairy-free Greek-style yogurt	Yes	Use nut-free granola
Ham and Cheese Super Spirals	Page 92	Use gluten-free pizza crust/dough	Use dairy-free cheese	Make sure pizza crust/dough is egg free	Yes
Rainbow Tortellini Salad	Page 94	Use gluten-free pasta	Use dairy-free Parmesan-style cheese	Make sure tortellini is egg free	Yes
Barbeque Chicken Biscuit Bombs	Page 96	Use gluten-free biscuit dough	Use dairy-free shredded cheese	Make sure biscuit dough is egg free	Yes
Dip-tastic Lunch with Homemade Hummus	Page 98	Use gluten-free pretzels or gluten-free crackers (if using)	Yes	Yes	Use sunflower seed butter or other nut-free butter
Five-Star Dinners					
One-Pot Mac and Cheese with Trees	Page 102	Use gluten-free pasta	Use unflavored, unsweetened dairy-free milk and dairy-free cheese	Yes	Yes
Chicken Fajita Burrito Bowls	Page 104	Yes	Use dairy-free Greek-style yogurt or dairy-free sour cream	Yes	Yes
Easy-Peasy Noodle Stir-Fry	Page 106	Use rice noodles or gluten-free noodles	Yes	Make sure packaged noodles are egg-free	Yes
Presto! Pesto Spaghetti	Page 108	Use gluten-free spaghetti	Use dairy-free Parmesan-style cheese and dairy-free mozzarella cheese (if using)	Yes	Use seeds (such as sunflower seeds) instead of almonds/nuts
Crispy Chicken Sammies	Page 110	Use gluten-free breadcrumbs and gluten-free buns	Use dairy-free unsweetened plain yogurt	Use an egg-free or vegan mayonnaise (or 3 tbsp [45 ml] additional yogurt)	Yes
Mini Deep-Dish Pizzas	Page 112	Use a gluten-free flour blend	Use dairy-free cheese	Yes	Yes
Mild-but-Mighty Chili with Easy Cheesy Cornbread	Page 115	Use a gluten-free cornbread mix or recipe	Omit sour cream/Greek yogurt or use dairy-free alternative; omit cheese or use dairy-free cheese	Make sure cornbread mix is egg-free	Yes
Ultimate Burgers with Toppings Bar	Page 118	Use gluten-free buns	Use dairy-free cheese	Use egg-free or vegan mayonnaise	Yes
Three-Cheese Lasagna	Page 120	Use gluten-free lasagna noodles or other gluten-free pasta that's been cooked	Use dairy-free ricotta and shredded cheese	Omit eggs (lasagna may not slice as well but still taste good)	Yes
Oven-Baked Corn Dogs	Page 122	Use a gluten-free flour blend	Use dairy-free milk	Yes	Yes

RECIPE NAME	PAGE NUMBER	GLUTEN-FREE	DAIRY-FREE	EGG-FREE	NUT-FREE
Shrimp California Roll Sushi Bowls	Page 124	Yes	Yes	Use egg-free or vegan mayonnaise	Yes
Superstar Chicken Pot Pie	Page 126	Use gluten-free pie crust	Use dairy-free milk, dairy-free butter and dairy-free pie crust	Make sure pie dough is egg-free; omit egg wash	Yes

Mic Drop Desserts

RECIPE NAME	PAGE NUMBER	GLUTEN-FREE	DAIRY-FREE	EGG-FREE	NUT-FREE
Chocolate Peanut Butter Crispy Treats	Page 130	Yes	Use dairy-free chocolate chips	Yes	Use sunflower seed butter or other seed butter
Cheesecake-Stuffed Strawberries	Page 132	Use gluten-free graham cracker	Use dairy-free cream cheese	Yes	Yes
No-Bake Cookie Dough Truffles	Page 134	Use almond flour or a gluten-free flour blend	Use dairy-free butter and dairy-free chocolate chips	Yes	Use heat-treated all-purpose flour in place of almond flour (see recipe for substitution measurements)
S'mores Brownie Bites	Page 136	Use gluten-free graham crackers and a gluten-free flour blend	Use dairy-free butter and dairy-free chocolate chips	Use a flax egg: 1 tbsp (10 g) ground flaxseed mixed with 3 tbsp (45 ml) water; use vegan marshmallows	Use sunflower seed butter or other nut-free butter
Pucker-Up Lemon Bars	Page 138	Use a gluten-free flour blend	Use dairy-free butter	No (substitutions not recommended)	Yes
Big and Chewy Chocolate Chip Cookies	Page 140	Use a gluten-free flour blend	Use dairy-free butter and dairy-free chocolate chips	Use a flax egg: 1 tbsp (10 g) ground flaxseed mixed with 3 tbsp (45 ml) water	Yes
Churro Pastry Twists with Chocolate Dipping Sauce	Page 143	Use gluten-free puff pastry if available	Use dairy-free butter, dairy-free chocolate and dairy-free milk	Make sure pastry dough is egg free	Yes
Disappearing Blueberry Cobbler	Page 146	Use a gluten-free flour blend	Use dairy-free butter, dairy-free milk and dairy-free ice cream (if using)	Yes	Yes
Secret Ingredient Chocolate "Dirt" Cups	Page 148	Use gluten-free chocolate cookies	Use dairy-free chocolate chips	Yes	Yes
Funfetti® Cupcakes with Easy Vanilla Frosting	Page 150	Use a gluten-free flour blend	Use dairy-free milk	No (substitutes not recommended)	Yes
Sweet Fruit Pizza with Sugar Cookie Crust	Page 152	Use a gluten-free flour blend	Use dairy-free butter and dairy-free cream cheese	Use 3 tbsp (45 ml) applesauce or a flax egg (see above for measurements)	Yes
Mini Apple Hand Pies	Page 154	Use gluten-free pie dough	Make sure pie dough is dairy-free	Make sure pie dough is egg free; use milk or water for top	Yes
Mint Chocolate Chip Ice Cream Cake	Page 157	Use gluten-free chocolate cookies (or gluten-free chocolate sandwich cookies)	Use canned full-fat coconut milk and sweetened condensed coconut milk	Yes	Yes

ACKNOWLEDGMENTS

Thank you to everyone at Page Street Publishing, including Meg, Rosie, Jamie and the marketing team. I know how much time and hard work you put into this book, and I couldn't appreciate it more. Thank you for the opportunity to help get more kids into the kitchen and cultivate a new generation of excellent cooks.

Thank you so much to my editor, Sarah. This book wouldn't have come to being without your initial idea and outreach. You have given me so much patient guidance through the book writing process, and I feel so lucky that we got to share an A&J King breakfast in person.

Michelle, your photographs truly brought my recipes to life. I can't thank you enough for getting through that crazy month of June with me (especially with your little one on the way). Your company, support and expertise were invaluable, and I really hope we can work together again in the future.

Mom and Dad, thank you for always checking in and being excited for the book along the way. Your support and love mean so much to me.

Kyle, thank you for being there with me through the ups and downs. You are the best dad to our boys, and I love doing this crazy life with you.

Donna, Norman, Breana and Jacob, I appreciate your support and kindness so much. I'm so lucky to have married into such a wonderful family.

Thank you to my honorary PR team and lead cheerleaders, Marissa and Katie. You are both so kind for always getting the word out about my blog, books and recipes.

Rebecca, thank you for all your help and encouragement through the process of creating this book. Your organization skills and friendship made the stressful times so much easier.

Taesha, thank you for being the "coworker" and friend I can vent to about life as well as brainstorm with about recipes. It was so nice having you and Allie in my corner throughout this project.

A big thank you to all my trusty kid recipe testers and their parents. You all were so dedicated to helping make this book the best it could be. It was so exciting to see the pictures of you trying out the recipes in your own kitchens, and I am so grateful for the time you spend giving me feedback and notes.

ABOUT THE AUTHOR

Heather Wish Staller is a recipe developer and cooking instructor who specializes in helping kids of all ages gain confidence and skills in the kitchen. A mother of two boys, she loves introducing children to the wonders of fresh and delicious food, and helping parents raise happy, healthy eaters. After going to Bowdoin College (where she met her husband), she fulfilled her lifelong dream of going to culinary school.

When she's not cooking, you can find her spending time with her family at their home by the beach outside Boston. Get more of Heather's recipes on her website, happykidskitchen.com, and join the wonderful community of food-loving parents and caregivers on Instagram at @heather.happykidskitchen.

INDEX